MW00445905

"A terrific book! I can't think of a m
faces right now than how to bring
traditions into the modern and pc
most urgent and far-reaching things we have to do, and this is a major
step in that direction."
—Ken Wilber, author of Integral Spirituality

"A vivid and inspiring reminder that growth and transformation on a
large-scale or global level are inseparable from honest and sometimes
painful reckoning of our flaws and failings on a personal level."
—Jack Canfield, coauthor of The Success Principles

"This book offers much hard-earned and valuable wisdom. His love
of Zen and his maturity has transformed Zen into a practice of the
heart."
— Jack Kornfield, author of Bringing Home the Dharma

"A very important contribution to the convergence of deep spiritual
practice and contemporary Western psychology, and a deeply honest,
self-revealing account of a Western Zen teacher's journey. As both a
therapist and a Zen teacher, I highly recommend this book to anyone
on the spiritual path, to therapists, and to all those interested in ex-
panding their understanding of themselves and their lives."
—Zen Master Nicolee Jikyo McMahon, Marriage and Family Therapist

"There's a lot of meat and marrow here, as well as things which might
stick in one's throat. *Ruination* can be a true friend with benefits, as
this candid story reveals. We who are imperfect can certainly sympa-
thize and even identify with Genpo Roshi's story and inner journey.
If you want a deep slice of American Zen life, from a teacher's point
of view, with all its ups and downs, twists and turns — beyond over-
idealized images — read this book."
—Lama Surya Das, author of Awakening the Buddha Within

"Like that lotus rising out of muddy water, the development of a Zen teacher is not an easy task, and as Genpo Roshi's book shows, the times of descending the mountain can be those of greatest self-discovery. We can be grateful that he has persevered and written this honest and generous account of his journey. I think it conveys the true spirit not only of his journey, but of his teacher's, my husband Maezumi Roshi, and of the Path we are all traveling in our own ways."

—*Martha Ekyo Maezumi, Artist and widow of Taizan Maezumi Roshi*

"Absolutely riveting! Genpo Roshi is a master storyteller and a master teacher and this book is alive with his vitality. Its message, and his journey, are both timely and universal. Traditional religions, and their leaders, must now learn to help people go through their own personal transformational processes. Many new paths are opening — many different journeys are becoming possible. Dennis Genpo Roshi has shown us his journey. Those who read this book can use his story to help them find their own paths."

—*Hal & Sidra Stone, Creators of Voice Dialogue (from the Foreword)*

"Most of what has been written in the West about Zen Buddhism focuses on climbing the path to enlightenment and standing on top of the mountain. However, what distinguishes Mahayana Buddhism from other spiritual traditions is that it stresses losing it all, coming down empty-handed from the peak of enlightenment back to the smelly swamps of everyday human life, as a crucial part of the spiritual process. This inspiring personal account of ascending and descending the mountain is one of the best books I have ever read about the struggle to become what Mahayana Buddhism calls a bodhisattva, a true human being."

—*Maurice Shonen Knegtel, Sensei, author of The Last Word of Zen*

"This book reads like a series of intimate fireside chats with a Zen teacher who is recounting what he has learned over 45 years of dedicated Zen practice. It skillfully weaves element of that process as well as traditional Zen koans. Unfolding a broad range of topics, including the complexities of the student-teacher, Big Mind and Abhidharma, and the future spiritual evolution of the human species."

—*Zen Master Jan Chozen Bays, author of The Vow-Powered Life*

Spitting Out the Bones

A Zen Master's 45 Year Journey

Spitting Out the Bones

A Zen Master's 45 Year Journey

D. Genpo Merzel

Foreword by Hal & Sidra Stone

PUBLISHING
SALT LAKE CITY

Book and cover design: Mark Esterman

Cover calligraphy (*enso*): Martha Ekyo Maezumi

For information contact:

BIG MIND PUBLISHING
32 WEST 200 SOUTH, #429
SALT LAKE CITY, UTAH 84101
www.bigmind.org

Library of Congress Control Number: 2016940640

ISBN 978-0-9771423-9-2 (pbk.)

Printed in the United States of America   10 9 8 7 6 5 4 3 2 1

Dedication

I dedicate this book to my great master Taizan Maezumi Roshi, who devoted his life to swallowing the whole fish and spitting out the bones in order that the Buddha-Dharma could take root here in the West.

Acknowledgements

I wish to thank first and foremost Mark Esterman Sensei for all the brilliant work, thoughtfulness and love he has put into this book. It literally would not be this book without him. I would also like to thank Charlotte Juul for her love and support, which have contributed so much to bringing me where I am today, and for helping me face some of my most deeply rooted patterns, which I would have loved to avoid. I am deeply grateful to my former wife, Stephanie Young Merzel for her love, courage and strength these past twenty years.

I also wish to thank my assistant Mary Ellen Sloan for her devotion and love and her amazing job keeping everything running so I could focus much of my time these past five years writing this book; Drs. Hal and Sidra Stone for being my mentors through this very challenging time; and Nicolee Jikyo McMahon Roshi for her help fine-tuning the manuscript as well her friendship the past thirty-five years.

There are a number of close friends and students to whom I wish to express my love and gratitude: Kamie Buddemeier, Paul Thielking, John Quigley, Joseph Hakim, Rob Velek, and Ivis Montenegro, among others who have been there consistently for me these past five years while I have taken time away from my teaching to focus on my own growth and development, and the writing of this book.

I would also like to express my appreciation and gratitude to the sixty-six Zen teachers who by taking what must have been a difficult stance, asking me to take a leave of absence from teaching Zen, helped me make a leap. I doubt that I would have done it without their ruthless compassion.

Lastly to Fillette Merzel for being my emotional support doggie and serving to relax and not judge me.

Deep bows of gratitude.

Contents

Contents

Foreword by Hal & Sidra Stone

When Genpo Roshi asked us to write a preface for his new book, it seemed as though it might require a good deal of effort. We are no longer young and, at this time of our lives, not only do we have many requests of this kind, but the focus required for writing is not as easy to come by as it was in the old days. Much to our delight, the reality was very different from our expectations. We both found this tale of Genpo Roshi's forty-five year journey absolutely riveting! He is a master storyteller and a master teacher and this book is alive with his vitality.

It seems to us that we are living in a time of exploding consciousness. And his is a story that belongs to these times. The world is changing and many people are personally changing in ways that are so dramatic as to be breathtaking. We have always found that the greatest learning — and much of the greatest teaching — comes from hearing someone's story. That is why we have always enjoyed our work. Listening to someone's story is always a gift: we invariably stand in awe of what has happened to people in their lives; what they have done with this; and, of course, where their journeys have taken them.

Genpo Roshi was born Dennis Merzel and the story is about the long transition from Dennis to Genpo and then the very difficult transition from Genpo to a new consciousness that has allowed him to stand in the world in a new and different way. Where he stands now more and more of the time, to use his own language, is at the Apex. From this place he has learned to embrace and value Dennis Merzel as well as Genpo Roshi. They have equal value and equal meaning.

This was not easy to accomplish. During a number of years of deep and difficult self-exploration he stayed true to his Buddhist training and lineage even as he explored the issues of his personal and professional life. He also embraced, or more accurately re-embraced Dennis, the man who lives life and loves life as an ordinary human being. These are a pair of opposites that remain central to his story as you will see as you read this book. What is particularly exciting to us is the fact that this is a story that belongs to all of us and, in reading about Genpo Roshi's psycho-spiritual adventures and search, we recognize that same process in ourselves.

Genpo Roshi in addition to having a profound knowledge of Zen, knows when and how to tell a story, and the many koans of the Zen Buddhist tradition come to life with his telling. Although we feel quite related to the Buddhist tradition, we actually know little about the actual teachings. So, for us, this book was a rich feast of Buddhist lore. We very much look forward to reading his stories of the Buddhist masters again, to following with him as he explores their complexities, and to savoring the subtleties he reveals.

Spitting Out the Bones is a powerful description of early Buddhist training. Dennis realized early on that the basic requirement of this stage of the training was that you must surrender to your teacher totally no matter how you might feel or how much you might disagree with him or her. To surrender was to swallow the teacher completely and digest him or her as best you could. At a later time you may spit out the bones. It is at this later time that you may determine what belongs to you and what doesn't belong to you.

Genpo raises some really serious questions about this teaching model. He gives many examples of how this didn't work for him at different points in his life. But he doesn't call it wrong and he doesn't call it right. He simply shares what happened to him and the conflicts he had then, and still has now about all of this. He is remarkably candid and it is like fresh air blowing in from the sea to listen to him talk about these kinds of conflicts with no sense of judgment at all.

In another place he raises an additional issue concerning the training of Zen teachers. He talks about the use of "the carrot" in training situations. This has to do with the practice of rewarding both students and teachers along the path with promotions; these give aspiring teachers greater status. This is a kind of hierarchical certification and it often creates real problems. At the same time, Genpo does not make this practice bad or say it should not be. He just shares how it has affected him and what it means to have this kind of power as a Roshi. How does this power affect the senior person in this kind of setting? How did he or she use this power? How does he or she make the decision to promote someone? Is this really a good way to teach and train people? You will not find a simple answer because there isn't any. You will find how it affected him, good and bad, and you are left with the issue as it applies to your own life.

The last chapters were of great interest to us because in this book, Genpo Roshi has given us a new and updated version of Big Mind. Big Mind is no longer a matter of exploring the Mind with a big M. It is no longer simply about the transpersonal aspects of the psyche. Big Mind now is the comprehensive exploration of the psyche as well as the spirit. It is about discovering all that you can about what is inside of you and how this affects the world outside. We quote a short paragraph from this chapter:

> These days I am much more interested in the Apex or the total triangle. I have named the left side the contracted dualistic self, the right side Big Mind or the non-dual, and the Apex Big Heart, or the Integrating Free-Functioning Human Being, or simply the Aware Self, or Me. Now I am more concerned that people have a Big Heart perspective and live from Big Heart, the Apex rather than remain in the impersonal non-dual transcendent or Absolute. I see this as true transcendence, which in my thinking includes and yet goes beyond both the relative and the absolute, the personal and the impersonal.

Genpo is no longer identified with a spiritual reality that drives people always towards the transcendent. Dennis Genpo talks about the Apex that he calls the Big Heart or the Integrating Free-Functioning Human Being or simply the Aware Self or Me. We would call this the Aware Ego Process. It doesn't matter what one calls it. Each of us comes to our own awareness and names things in our own way because that is just the way creativity works. What is essential is that Dennis Genpo is now the new Sailing Master of his own ship and both Dennis and Genpo are now well represented. Whatever name we may give to the Apex doesn't really make any difference. It has gone beyond the duality of the transcendent and the ordinary.

We believe that this book is a game-changer. This book is about an evolution that is going on amongst spiritual teachers of many persuasions. Since Dennis Genpo Roshi is a Zen Buddhist, we believe that this book is going to have a particularly powerful impact on many of the Zen Buddhist communities, but its message, and his journey, are both timely and universal.

Traditional religious forms have lost their power to heal. Traditional religious forms must now learn how to help people discover how to go through their own personal transformational processes in their own unique fashions. To do that, the leaders must go through their own personal transformational processes.

Many new paths are opening —many different journeys are becoming possible. Dennis Genpo Roshi has shown us his journey; he has shown us his own creative process. Those who read this book can use his story to help them find their own paths. And we are sure that he will be working on this process and will continue this journey with the same vitality, dedication, and enthusiasm for the remainder of this life ... and beyond.

Hal Stone, Ph.D. & Sidra Stone, Ph.D.
Albion, CA
September, 2015

SPITTING OUT THE BONES

1

Spitting Out the Bones

"Spitting out the bones." I remember the first time I heard this expression, from my elder Dharma brother Bernie Tetsugen Glassman. It was towards the end of 1972, he and I were sitting in the front seat of his car, waiting to pick up his son Marc from school. I had only recently come to live at the Zen Center of Los Angeles; he had already been studying with Zen Master Taizan Maezumi for many years. Though he was Roshi's senior student, five and a half years older than me with a family and a much more settled life, we had struck up the beginnings of a lifelong friendship and had a lot more in common than our outward differences might have suggested. Both of us had an independent streak coupled with a capacity for great self-discipline, focus, and hard work, he as an aerospace engineer with a Ph.D. in mathematics, myself as an accomplished swimmer and water polo player. Both of us Brooklyn-born Jewish boys transplanted in Southern California, we shared a single-minded commitment to Zen practice and an absolute dedication to our teacher, Maezumi Roshi.

It was Maezumi Roshi's teaching that Bernie had heard over and over again and was now passing on to me for the first but certainly not the last time: "You have to swallow the whole fish, and then spit out the bones. That's our practice." We both really took it to heart and made it central to our practice. Swallow the whole fish. Don't judge Roshi, don't evaluate, don't make distinctions, right wrong, good, bad, any of that. Just swallow the whole fish. Then we could spend the rest of our lives spitting out the bones.

That's what both of us have continued to do, and I think Maezumi Roshi's repeating it over and over made us feel perfectly fine about it. Over the years people have criticized the two of us for the ways we are transmitting the teachings, as not true Zen, not the original fish. So I remain grateful that Roshi not only gave us permission but encouraged us to spit out the bones, because he believed the practice of Zen needs to adapt to the culture it is in.

Spitting out the bones is essential to the process of transplanting the Dharma, the Buddha's teachings, in a new continent, a new culture. This wasn't just Maezumi Roshi's teaching; in my opinion it is characteristic of Zen as it has moved from culture to culture. Because, as Roshi told us again and again, he was Japanese — it was in his blood, he was born and grew up in a Japanese Zen Temple — we Americans were not. We're all conditioned by our upbringing, our culture and our circumstances. He couldn't develop a Western Zen. It is our generation in our culture, and the generations following us that are going to have to do it. For Zen to truly take root in this Western world we will have to spit out the bones.

To take the metaphor a step further, once we choose the fish we have to bite into it, chew it well, swallow it, and of course digest it. The part we digest is totally absorbed into our bloodstream and cells and becomes one with our whole body. That's what I am calling the essence. The part that is not digested and is spat out, I am calling the bones. We used to say it would probably take us the rest of our lives to separate the bones from the essence of Zen itself. I know that's been a part of my evolution, my work and my teaching, for the past forty-five years.

*   *   *

But which is the bones, and which is the essence? Which is the Japanese, the culture, and which is Zen? What I'm seeing is, all the forms, and all our ideas about Zen, that's the bones. Then there's the essence, I don't know what to call it other than the meat that is digested. It has nothing to do with specific forms or practices, with our beliefs or concepts. It's not particularly Japanese, Chinese, Korean or Indian.

For Maezumi Roshi, when he came to America the meat was Zen Buddhism as he knew it, as a Japanese in a Japanese culture. He was born in a Zen Temple in Japan and had studied and absorbed the whole world of Buddhism from the time of the Buddha. So he too had to work with the question of how to spit out the bones. He talked to us about spitting out what we were getting from the Japanese culture, but he didn't seem to be completely at peace with what he himself was doing. For example, when he gave ordinations he would take his wedding ring off because he felt as a married man he shouldn't be performing ordinations for monks or nuns. He made many changes from the way he was trained, but I am not sure that he didn't have a lot of inner conflict about it.

Sometimes in order to get a clear view of the situation you're in you have to step out of it. I remember back when I first started going to Europe in 1982, I was able to get a clearer perspective on America and its culture. I could see just how puritanical American culture is and how this came out in so many uptight ways. Europe was so much more relaxed in many ways, especially around sexuality. When I returned after a year in Europe I also saw how focused we Americans were on money, even around the dinner table, even in a spiritual setting.

When I went to Korea in '81, I got a clearer perspective on Japanese Zen, because Korean Zen was so totally different from pretty much everything that I took as Zen. I remember the first time I went to one of their monasteries, the monks' slippers and sandals were strewn all over the place. It was just a sloppy mess. They'd leave their slippers in the dirt, then they'd step on others' slippers so they didn't get their feet dirty, and then step up on the deck where it was clean.

In Japan you would never ever just throw your slippers down and step on other peoples' slippers to get inside. Then, when I got into the meditation hall, the *zendo*, everybody was sitting facing towards the Buddha. They were all seated in one row, though not in a straight line. Even their posture was very relaxed and not stiff like the Japanese Soto Zen posture. To me, Zen had straight lines and straight spines. I had to see that everything I took as Zen wasn't Zen, it was Japanese Zen, and there was a Korean Zen, which was definitely different.

The differences in Buddhism can be about matters that are

much deeper than form, and go right to the heart of what we think of as Buddhism. In the Theravada tradition, the oldest school of Buddhism, as it was explained to me by the monks I met in Thailand in 1990, the teaching wasn't about awakening; it was more about the rules and regulations. For us in Zen, the Buddha was to be realized within ourselves. In the Southeast Asian countries the Buddha is the historical Buddha, not what is inherent within each of us. I make a distinction between Buddha and Buddhism, the "ism" part being another thing we have to spit out. To me Buddha is our very embodiment of our True Nature.

So when we were training under Maezumi Roshi back in the '70's and '80's, it was a lot about meticulously copying the Japanese forms and almost becoming Japanese. At some point I even started talking and looking quite Japanese. My inflections and manners of speech sounded so much like my teacher's that many times I was mistaken for a Japanese, even by Japanese people, as well as by Westerners. At times it seemed to me that for some people it was more about form than about true understanding. Not that I'm making it wrong; we were studying with a Japanese Zen Master. As Roshi always said, "first learn my way then it is up to you successors to change the form and Westernize it appropriately." If we hadn't swallowed the whole fish first, it would have been even harder to know what to spit out and what to leave in.

I remember Roshi always saying, "It's all *upaya*," all skillful means. I agree with him. However, everything we become identified with becomes part of our identity, and we become attached to that new identity. So if I consider myself Genpo Roshi, or I consider myself a Zen Buddhist, or I consider myself a monk or a priest, a teacher or whatever I am identified with, the more I've invested in that identity — and for me now it's over forty-five years of investment — the harder it is to let go of it.

The Zen practices that we were most familiar with when I was training, came out of a Japanese, male, monastic culture. The ancient Chinese were different. They led a hermit-like life, but they didn't have that same monastic framework as in Japan. The early masters and their followers are often depicted wandering in the mountains or living deep within them. In fact our impression that they were wild and eccentric was what appealed to many of us about Zen back in those days.

*　*　*

One thing I've been adamant about for some time is not to get attached to the idea that a specific practice is 'it,' whether it's sitting meditation (*zazen*) or chanting or bowing or Big Mind, or whatever. Because then if we're not doing what we think of as practice we don't feel OK or good about ourselves. This is a pitfall J. Krishnamurti pointed out very perceptively — how we believe that because we meditate or we do yoga or some other practice we're OK, and if we don't do it we're not OK. It's not dealing with our life as it is.

Actually, I see this as one of the points where I'm critical of some of the followers of Zen Master Dogen. I love and appreciate much of his teaching, but I think it's led some people and even certain schools of Zen to believe that if you're not sitting you're not practicing, that sitting *is* practice. It's true that sitting is practice, and practice is sitting, but that doesn't mean that sitting has to take a particular form such as the lotus posture. Or that if we are not sitting then we are not practicing Zen, or that others are not practicing because they're not sitting.

In a world that has much greater problems, such attachment to particular forms can become very narrow and small-minded. Form does have its place and can be very helpful and supportive — at the proper time, place and amount under the right conditions —for us students of the Way who need some structure and discipline, not necessarily Japanese, to assist us in overcoming certain unhealthy habitual patterns. The key is distinguishing what is essential from bones that are to be spit out.

From one perspective it is true that practice is enlightenment and enlightenment is practice. However we shouldn't forget that whatever we do from morning till night is practice, is enlightenment. Bowing, walking, cleaning standing up and sitting down are all "It." It has gotten to the point where in some Zen communities the thinking is if we are not doing sitting meditation many hours a day we aren't practicing true Zen.

I think that goes back to our experience with the great Japanese teachers who came to America in the early days. The occasions where they could introduce and present their teachings were the intensive retreats, *sesshins*, they conducted, so for many of us Westerners that became our idea of Zen practice. Sitting ten hours a day or more was Zen, and everything else was not Zen. So we would come and we would practice Zen, do a retreat, then go back into our life, which didn't look or feel like our idea of practice. This to me is one of the bones we are spitting out. What constitutes practice, what constitutes Zen if it's not our life itself and every moment?

* * *

Another bone from the Japanese tradition we were raised in that I feel we need to spit out is the inability to think differently from our teacher, or to go against the teacher's inner attachments. In the time I studied with Maezumi Roshi there were a lot of things we students didn't feel good about, even disapproved of, but we wouldn't discuss them with him. We wouldn't be transparent with him. You just couldn't do that. At the time we just accepted it. Looking back, it might have been better for him and for us, no matter what the short-term consequences, if we had been truthful with each other, but that really wasn't the way, particularly the Japanese way.

In hindsight I would say it would have been better, but frankly I don't think it was possible to be open with him and be taken seriously as a student capable of receiving Dharma transmission, *Shiho*, and advancing to being a successor and teacher. Just before receiving transmission at the end of September 1980, I went to conduct a retreat in Phoenix, Arizona, and during that retreat I had a profound experience. I was giving a koan lecture, a *teisho*, on the Sixth Zen Patriarch, and in the lecture I became one with the Sixth Patriarch. I mean, it was like I *was* him, I was in the abbot's room receiving the transmission from the Fifth Patriarch, and it was a total body experience. I broke down, sobbing, right in the middle of my talk.

When I came back to Roshi, I wanted to tell him two things. First, I had this experience of being the Sixth Patriarch, that I *am* the lineage, that's who I am! He was furious with me. "DON'T FORGET ME," he demanded, "I'm the connection, I'm the coupling, I'm what connects you to the lineage." The second thing I hesitated to say, because I knew his reaction was going to be negative, was that I was having doubts about being worthy of receiving transmission. But I decided to go for it, and the moment I said it he did exactly what I was afraid he would do. "NO TRANSMISSION FOR YOU! YOU'RE HAVING DOUBTS. I'M GOING TO CALL IT OFF!"

I did receive transmission a week or two later as planned, however at the time it seemed he would not allow me or others to be honest, we couldn't doubt. The whole practice is about questioning and doubting — great doubt, great enlightenment, little doubt little enlightenment, no doubt no enlightenment — yet it seemed he didn't really leave room for doubt. And I don't think it was a negative doubt. Am I worthy of being a Successor in the Buddhist lineage? No, I'm not worthy. Why didn't he just say, 'You know, it's true you're not worthy,' and we go ahead? But it was so difficult to be transparent with him and share misgivings, or any kind of doubt in oneself, or even just criticism of oneself. It seemed at least to most of us that it wasn't allowed.

There were a lot of things we students couldn't disagree with our teacher about, but we wouldn't want to share it with him, because there wasn't room to be personal, or what might be called transparent. I remember one time we were in his house, he was clipping my hair — we took turns of course — and complaining about how American students think they can be your 'buddy.' I felt terrible. It would have been different if I'd been clipping his hair, but while he's clipping mine he's telling me, "You can't be buddy with teacher, must be vertical, must be teacher-student." That would be getting into the personal, and he didn't have space for that. He also didn't have much patience with what we might call transparency or honesty. 'Stupid honesty,' he called it, 'idiot's honesty.'

It struck me a few years ago that the time I really connected with him was in 1972-73, when I moved into the Zen Center and he was having so much trouble after being divorced from his first wife. His pain had made him uncharacteristically open and accessible. He had just become a master, and his vulnerability was still very apparent. That's when I fell in love with him and we really bonded.

His big criticism of me as a teacher was that I interacted with students in a way that was too egalitarian, too much on the same, horizontal level. I can see now how right he was and how important it is for us teachers to be clear about boundaries. As teachers we need to be able to engage with students on a horizontal level, but always respecting appropriate boundaries in the context of teacher-student. We must be discerning about position, place, time and amount. When we are not, there is a strong chance for confusion and misuse of power.

In April of 1978, when Maezumi Roshi went to Japan for Tetsugen Sensei's *Zuisse*, the ceremony of Appreciating the Founders of the Soto School of Zen, he left me in charge of the Zen Center and had me doing formal interviews with students for the first time. These are supposed to be private interviews between a student and a Zen Master who has received final seal of approval, *Inka*. But I was not yet a teacher, a *Sensei*, and hadn't yet completed koan study, though I was very close, and finished the following year. There had been a big issue between Roshi and his teacher Koryu Roshi about doing interviews before one is a Roshi, so Maezumi Roshi didn't want Koryu Roshi knowing about me holding interviews back at ZCLA.

Then when he came back a number of people told him how much they appreciated me holding interviews, that I was so personal. He summoned me into his private room, and he was irate. "ZEN IS NOT ABOUT BEING PERSONAL, IT'S BEING IMPERSONAL," he said, and really came down on me for being too personal, too horizontal. That was often his complaint with me, that I was 'too much buddy-buddy' with the students. Of course now I can see his point; but it has taken me many years, several rises and falls, to be clear about the very sensitive relationship between student and teacher.

A few years ago, in 2011, I was talking to a group of students about my relationship with Maezumi Roshi. I recalled that in all the nearly twenty-four years I was with him, there were only four times after '73, maybe five, when he seemed to drop the role of teacher and we really connected on a horizontal, heart level. It was so rare for him to step out of that role, and for me the whole horizontal was missing, the love, the heart connection that I had experienced earlier.

We did have a heart connection, but we seldom met at that place. For me it was only while I was traveling with him, usually in Europe, that we would really connect in that personal, intimate way. There's a photo I'm very fond of, taken of the two of us sitting together on a train coming back from Poland to Amsterdam, both of us smiling, relaxed. That was one of those rare moments when we were meeting on a heart level, not just as teacher and student.

❉   ❉   ❉

I've known since 1971 that in my life what has come easily for me is the spiritual, or you could say the absolute side. But the other side — the personal relationships, the relative — that can't be ignored. When I talk about this, I like to use the image of a triangle: the relative or the personal is at one end of the base, the impersonal or the absolute at the other end. The apex includes and transcends the absolute and the relative, and manifests as the integration of the two, just as the Sangha, the Buddhist community, embodies the harmony of Buddha and Dharma.

Sangha
Apex

Buddha   **Dharma**
Real, absolute reality /   Apparent, relative reality /
impersonal   personal

Much of the work I'm doing on myself these days is about the personal and relational, because I know that I've tended to abide, or take refuge, more in the Buddha, the absolute, than in the Dharma, the relative, these past forty-five years. The transcendent, the realization, the awakening comes easily for me. It's the personal and relational — how, as uniquely different and vulnerable individuals, do we connect and relate to each other in healthy and positive ways? That's the challenge for me and maybe for all of us, perhaps it's our big koan in these times.

In that spirit, I think another bone to be spit out is seeing personal relationships and family as secondary to the Dharma, both in teaching and in Dharma relationships, and considering family as not Dharma. What was transmitted within the tradition is that somehow Sangha excluded family, and this understanding caused families a lot of suffering. In my view, family is Dharma.

For me this understanding of Sangha as including both the relational and the transcendent is the West's contribution to the Three Treasures and needs to be embraced by us today. I believe it represents a major — and inevitable — turning point in the evolution of Buddhism, which I see as the Fourth Turning of the Dharma Wheel. If it is truly going to happen we are going to need to make Sangha more broad and inclusive and see everyone and everything as Buddha-Dharma.

The understanding of Sangha, of who is included or excluded, has been evolving ever since the time of the historical Buddha. These different understandings are a pile of bones that have been discarded in different ages and places. According to Maezumi Roshi, for some years in the early period of the historical Buddha's teaching, Sangha included only the male monks who had received ordination. Women were not allowed to become nuns and to join the Sangha. In the Theravada school it is still true that only ordained monks and nuns are permitted to be called Sangha.

Now I see Sangha as all beings, not just those who are in so-called Buddhism. I think there's going to be a day when, just as we now see all races, all people regardless of status, position or means as human beings, we're going to see that animals too share much more of the qualities we regard as essentially human. I mean, we're going to see all creatures and all beings and all life and everything as equal, different, unique and included as Sangha, as Buddha-Dharma, and worth rescuing. Our vision now just seems too narrow.

To me Sangha really means the harmony and inseparability of Buddha-Dharma. Using the analogy of the triangle, I see Buddha (the absolute) and Dharma (the relative) as the two corners of the triangle, and Sangha as the Apex, which is the manifested Buddha-Dharma. In fact we can't separate the Buddha from the Dharma, and we can't separate the absolute from the relative, they are truly inseparable. There is no absolute apart from the relative and no relative apart from the absolute. That's the harmony we're living out, or working through, and you could say our koan, or our practice is, how do we live as the Buddha-Dharma, as Sangha?

*　　*　　*

We can look at practice, or Buddha-Dharma — and I think the word practice can be misleading, it's life — we can look at it in two ways. One way is as if there's an ideal of Buddhism, or an ideal of being enlightened, or awakened or conscious. I think most people who seek to follow a spiritual path are still trying to become that ideal perfect person. The second way is to think, What I am is *this*, and I'm working on refining what I am. Rather than looking at what I should become, I'm working with who I am.

From the perspective of the Apex, which includes and embraces both the relative and the absolute, the human and the being, we see clearly that we are perfect within our imperfection and imperfect within our perfection. And yet, understanding that we are already complete and whole, we still have lots of work and practice to do in refining ourselves and working on our shadows and stuck places.

In Zen we have many koans about this: 'Wipe as you will, you can never wipe the dust away' — because to begin with there is no dust and yet there is endless refining. Or the koan about Mahakashapa and Ananda when Ananda, after years at the side of the Buddha and then with Mahakashapa, asks, 'When the Buddha transmitted the robe and bowl to you, was there anything else that he transmitted?' — still believing he was missing something.

What we work on is our life, not some ideal. And a good part of that work is spitting out the bones, which takes tremendous faith and trust, trust in oneself as the Buddha-Dharma. If we are still judging ourselves — Is this Buddhism or not Buddhism? Am I living up to this ideal or not? — it's because of a lack of deep realization and a lack of true faith, not in something but in no-thing-ness, *sunyata* or Buddha Nature. This realization is what brings out the faith and trust that is already inherent in oneself as Buddha-Dharma. If you truly realize that and are living it, everything else is bones.

2

Submission, Power and Empowerment

As students of Maezumi Roshi in those early days at the Zen Center of Los Angeles, one aspect of our practice that was considered essential, at least until I left there in 1984, was submission to our teacher. The way I appreciated this was that the teacher was the living embodiment of the Buddha-Dharma, so a true student of the Way, especially one who aspired to be a genuine lineage holder, needed to submit completely to the Buddha-Dharma manifested in the form of the teacher.

I did this myself from 1972 to 1995, and probably held on to that view for forty years. That has certainly changed in the past few years. I started to look at it closely in 2011, and it remains the most challenging piece of the whole fish I swallowed in committing myself to Zen practice, but I've moved away from thinking it's essential in the form that we experienced it back then at ZCLA.

For me, submission to a teacher was something I intuitively felt I needed to do. It was a conscious decision. I remember it clearly: the day in September of 1972 I was crossing Normandie Avenue from the apartment where I lived when I first came to ZCLA, on my way to early morning zazen. There I was, back in LA, when I realized the last place in the world I really wanted to be was Los Angeles, and that if I was going to be there I was going to completely give up my power and my own authority and entrust it to my Zen Master, Maezumi Roshi.

I'd already had numerous experiences of what in Zen we call dropped off body/mind, and I was certain that I was Buddha and that others were too, only they had not realized it yet. I saw myself as the Buddha, God, the creator as well as all creations, but at the same time I sensed that this was too much for my immature ego to handle. I remember thinking I needed somebody to just pulverize my ego, and this was the only way I could see to make that happen.

So between stepping off the curb and getting to the other side of the street, I made the conscious choice that I was going to truly submit, all my power and everything, to Roshi. Now, more than forty years later and with the benefit of 40/40 hindsight, I see that I wouldn't be who I am today had I not done so. There have been many payoffs from that choice; however, there has also been a price.

*　*　*

The very word submission evokes the specter of blind obedience and cult-like abuse of unchecked power. However, it's obvious that someone who's not open and receptive cannot receive whatever is to be transmitted. There has to be space in the container to pour in something new. One has to be empty if one is to be filled. To submit is to put oneself under, like a glass under the tap. You can't put it above or to the side. It has to go under in order to receive. And at some point it is not enough to be a glass with a bottom, we must become bottomless, like a conduit or hose connected to the tap, so that the water flows through.

That is our practice, to be such a conduit. The Dharma flows through the conduit into another container, or better still, a new conduit. So in our Lineage Chart it flows as a red line through each new conduit/successor and then returns to the source, then again back through the lineage in an endless circle.

In Zen the view as I personally understand it is that we have to submit to an actual living teacher. Submitting to an ideology or a historical figure doesn't work, because in doing so we are only submitting to our own interpretation of those ideas or our projections of who the historical person was. It's like doing open heart surgery on oneself, which is definitely problematic.

This is not to say that submitting to a living teacher does not also present problems. For one thing, as students we get attached to our projections and our idealized image of our teacher. We take what the teacher is saying as truth, not as a view or opinion that can be questioned and grappled with. When I look back on my life, I see I did that too. The Buddha himself cautioned his followers not to accept even his words without questioning them thoroughly. Still, it has taken me a long time as a teacher to get to the place where I can say that I feel everything is just my view or opinion based on my life experiences and my understanding of the teachings. This too is part of the never-ending process of chewing and digesting the whole fish, of discerning what is our personal stuff and what is genuine teaching, what is merely copied from our teacher and what is true to our experience.

The rationale for submission is that without letting go of one's own ideas and beliefs, one cannot truly receive the teachings. How can we fully embody the teaching if we do not drop or empty ourselves of all our deeply held concepts and beliefs? However, that rationale raises a critical question: can we really drop our sense of what is true or right without losing some essential element of our integrity? Can the student be open and receptive, and yet not allow him- or herself to be subjected to a misuse of power? There can be a very fine line between good teaching and what we might consider misuse of power.

✳   ✳   ✳

In the Japanese tradition, the appreciation of submission is deeply rooted in samurai culture, and is often illustrated by the analogy of sword making. Steel is heated in red hot coals, then pounded with a hammer, then plunged into cold water and back into the fire, over and over again. In the teacher-student relationship, the effects of this process are not so clear-cut.

In my own case, I can see where I dropped some of my own values and healthy boundaries in surrendering to my teacher. I can also see where I hurt some students who had submitted to me. It has taken me many years to sort this out for myself and it is something I am still working on.

Of course there are two perspectives, the swordsmith's and the sword's. To the steel it may seem abusive to be scorched, beaten, and plunged into ice cold water again and again until its impurities are burned out and it is honed into a flawless razor-sharp sword. From the swordsmith's perspective it is the best way to produce a beautiful, lethal blade.

In my experience as a student there were many instances which in retrospect years later I may consider my teacher's misuses of his power, which from his perspective most likely appeared as absolutely necessary to make me into a worthy successor. One such incident occurred early in our time together. Back around 1973, a couple of students were pressuring Maezumi Roshi to buy some barren land for a future monastery in the high desert mountains up in Ojai California. He was feeling pushed, but reluctantly agreed to drive to Ojai from LA to look at the place, and asked me to accompany them as the driver.

When we got there, and while the other students went off to walk the property, Roshi and I opened a six pack of beer we had brought with us for lunch. As we drank and the other students were wandering around, he suddenly turned to me and said, "Let's go." I said I'd whistle to signal them to return. He said, "No, let's go!" I asked him to let me honk the horn to call them back, and again he said, "No! Let's go!" I drove him the hour and a half back to the Zen Center, feeling horrible and guilty all the long way home. Of course when we got back I sent someone after them. From my perspective, and I am sure theirs, this was absolutely a misuse of power; from Roshi's he was teaching them and possibly me a lesson: don't push him, he is the teacher and we are the students.

Twenty years later, when I was living and teaching in Oregon near my children and their mother, my former wife Hobai, Roshi demanded that I move out of the Pacific Northwest to make space for another of his successors, my Dharma sister who was already living in the Portland area. I had said that I did not want to move further away from my kids than I already was, which was forty minutes by car. He insisted that I put the property up for sale and wanted me to move to Europe, that my being in the same state, even in the Pacific Northwest, didn't give her ample room to develop her Sangha. I argued with him that I didn't want to move to

Europe, it was way too far from my children. "If you see your kids even once a year," he said, "it is enough!"

For Roshi this may have been a good teaching, to me it felt like a misuse of his power. In hindsight I can see how coming from two very different cultures we had two very different ideas about Dharma. For him, with his Japanese samurai Zen heritage, family was not Dharma, students and successors were Dharma. For me, as a Westerner and with a Jewish heritage, family is Dharma. By 1995 I realized Roshi and I had very different understandings about what is or is not Dharma, but In '93 I still adhered to the belief that ultimately my job and responsibility was to submit to my teacher. That is why I compromised my values by leaving my children and moving from Portland to Salt Lake City, a decision which I regret to this day.

＊　＊　＊

Submission, power, and empowerment within the teacher-student relationship — the whole subject is fraught with questions we need to look at as carefully and honestly as we can. First of all, for most of us submission has intensely negative connotations. We think of it as a total loss of our own power, coming from weakness, from giving up and defeat. But in fact we don't submit from a weak place. True submission comes from a very powerful and empowering decision, from within us, not from outside. Paradoxical as it may sound, we have to empower ourself to submit.

That is what happened to me in 1972 in the middle of Normandie Avenue the moment I decided to hand over my power, my autonomy, to Maezumi Roshi. It was an empowering moment for me, because all of a sudden I took possession of my power and chose to submit to another human being. Owning my power and consciously turning it over to him really allowed the whole process to begin.

This dynamic became clearer to me a year later during the year-end retreat at ZCLA in December of 1973. Tetsugen, who was the head monk, was called in for a rush job at McDonnell-Douglas. He was working seventy-two hours that week and couldn't be in the retreat. I had just become a monk in October, so I was the newest of about a dozen of Maezumi Roshi's monks. Not all, but a good ten of them were present for the week-long retreat.

One day during a lunch break I'm relaxing in my back yard getting some sun, and I'm thinking this retreat is kind of powerless, there's no juice in it, no energy, it's like — dead. All our other retreats had been very powerful, and I'm wondering, what's going on? What's wrong, what can we do? Then I realized it was because Tetsugen wasn't there. He was the one empowered, he was the head monk, the one with authority We all respected him, and he would bring that spirit into the retreats and inspire us. But he was gone, and nobody was doing it.

So I started to think, there's this senior monk, more senior than me, maybe I ask him to do it. And I realized, well, if he could he would. Then I went down the line, through the other people in the retreat, and I thought, well, if they could they would. So what do I do now? I realized I had to step up to the plate. So I went back into the zendo that afternoon and boldly sat not in my own place facing the wall, but in Tetsugen's seat, the head monk's, facing everybody. I started encouraging people to sit stronger, and walking with the 'waking-up stick,' the *kyosaku*.

That evening in my private interview with Roshi, *dokusan*, I asked him, 'Is there anybody who needs encouragement?' In those days we pushed people hard to practice. 'Anybody that needs some incentive — shouting, the stick?' He looked at me and said, 'Why are you asking me? You're in charge of the zendo.'

That was very empowering. But it would not have happened if I had not first stepped up and taken the role of leader. Then he was able to empower me, and after that the other students did as well. First we have to step up to the position, and if we're not ready or willing to do so, even if an external authority puts us in a position of power, we're not really going to feel empowered and act accordingly. This is something we can't just learn intellectually, we have to experience it to truly know it.

It's been pointed out to me that this is something we're learning about here in the West through studies of organizations, but it's all there in our Buddhist teachings, and has been for 2500 years. In empowerment ceremonies like offering the Buddhist Precepts, *Jukai,* or ordination, *Shukke Tokudo,* the teacher actually steps up to sit in the seat of the Buddha, and then when the students or recipients come in, they make their initial bows which empower the teacher to take the place of the Buddha in empowering them to be Buddha.

I had another vivid, I would even say visceral, insight into empowerment right after I first became a Zen teacher. I received transmission as a Dharma successor and teacher from Maezumi Roshi in September of 1980, but he had actually started having me hold *daisan,* private interviews between a teacher and a student, in April of 1978, prior to my empowerment. I was stepping into the role of guiding other students, of being a teacher, and in that role when people come for formal interviews — very often beginning by bowing before us — we can get inflated with the position, take it in, and feel, Wow, I'm really great, that people are bowing to me. Or we can kind of reject it, thinking we don't deserve it, putting ourself down.

After Dharma transmission I was no longer sitting there as myself, as Genpo, but as Buddha and the entire tradition and lineage. That allowed me to not get inflated in my own ego. There was an inflation, I'll come back to that. But I didn't take it personally. Instead I thought, 'I am sitting in this position in the place of the Buddha, embodying the lineage, trying to do whatever I can to help the person in front of me. But it's not about me. I am just a conduit for this tradition.'

So when I started holding formal interviews in '78, I would never keep my eyes open at the moment people came in and made their prostrations. I'd keep my eyes closed, because it was too much for me to handle. I tried to prevent my ego's becoming inflated by kind of denying that they were bowing to me, by closing my eyes. But two and a half years later, the day after I received transmission, while I was doing interviews I noticed my eyes were open, and I realized, 'Oh, they're open because these people are not bowing to me. They're bowing to the Buddha and the entire lineage. It's not me, so I don't need to take this on personally, and I don't need to get inflated or feel I need to deflect it.'

Still, it was not until 2004, twenty-four years later, that I really got what Dharma transmission is all about. While doing the transmission ceremony for Niko Tydeman, one of my Dutch successors, I got that this ceremony is actually giving birth to Buddhas, that there is something in this esoteric transmission that is really real. For twenty-four years I had loved the ceremony and conducted it many times with deep respect, but without a sense of its true import. I'd read the script, repeat the prescribed motions, and ... OK, now it's done. This time however, I got that it is real, it's really giving birth to a Buddha who can now give birth to other Buddhas.

So giving the Buddhist Precepts is one thing, but Dharma transmission is something else. In the Precepts ceremony we give birth to a baby Buddha. In transmission we're giving birth to Mahavairochana Buddha, who can actually give birth to other Buddhas. And there's something very real about it. It's not just stepping in and sitting down on the high seat of Mahavairochana Buddha, taking its place. *Now I am Mahavairochana Buddha,* as the chant goes: "Now I am Mahavairochana Buddha sitting on this lotus flower seat, surrounded by ten thousand lotus blossoms and on every blossom one thousand Shakyamuni Buddhas appear." That is a lot of Buddhas — and a lot of power.

Then I think what can happen, at least what happened to me, is that I got stuck in the identification with Mahavairochana Buddha. And this, as all the great masters such as Ummon, Joshu and Tozan have warned us, is a dangerous place to get stuck — dangerous not only for the one empowered as Buddha, but also for those who follow or study from that person.

* * *

As students we see power embodied in our teacher and we want what he or she has. We seek it but seldom admit that we do, even to ourselves, especially in the spiritual world where it is not considered OK to crave power. However, it is only realistic to acknowledge that most of us begin this practice with a gaining idea, what Chogyam

Trungpa Rinpoche called spiritual materialism. Mixed in with our desire for pure Dharma, and often superseding it, is a desire for recognition from the teacher, for something we can take out into the world, to feel powerful and acknowledged by others. To gain it we will do our utmost to get close and intimate with our teacher.

This craving for recognition and power is not necessarily a bad thing. I believe we all have it to some degree, but when it is unacknowledged and repressed, it can operate covertly in unhealthy and immature ways. Our desire for the teacher's recognition can be coming from our egoistic need to be number one, to be seen as special, and can lead to the competitive games with fellow students which bring up so much jealousy and envy. Our willingness to do our utmost to please the teacher can easily be confused with true submission.

Of course there are all kinds of power. Scientifically speaking, power is the capability to effect change, measured by the rate of that change. The greater the power, the faster the change. Zen's historic name, the Sudden School, implies that there is great power inherent in the practice — a sudden change such as a great awakening implies enormous power.

There's also power in knowledge, there's power in creating fear. There's power in position. There's power in having something that others want, in this case the teacher having something the student wants. It could be power, it could be calm, peacefulness. It could be wisdom, or love and clarity, it could be authority. It could be the Buddha-Dharma, it could be happiness. It could be many things. But to the student it looks like the teacher is embodying what I want, and therefore I give him or her power over me, because to get what I want I somehow have to make myself available for it. That's where we realize we need to submit to receive it.

A great deal of power comes with Dharma transmission. That was my personal experience when I received transmission in 1980 and also what I have observed in my Dharma successors. To identify oneself as all the Buddhas and particularly Mahavairochana Buddha is very empowering. To identify oneself as the parent of all Buddhas is power, and the responsibility that comes with it needs to be understood, but often isn't. It took me twenty-four more years to realize what this really meant. In hindsight I see that this realization drove an even deeper identification as Mahavairochana Buddha.

As teachers we are empowered to awaken others, to help give their lives meaning and purpose, and hopefully empower them to work towards the liberation of others. But power can certainly also be used negatively for one's own sake. We may consciously or unconsciously be fulfilling some of our own unacknowledged and unconscious needs. Power can be inebriating and addictive, and most of us certainly do not want to lose it once we have it.

I have seen how both I and others react when we are with our own teacher after we have acquired the power that transmission confers. When we successors of Maezumi Roshi were with him we seemed to feel we lost our power and we became smaller again in his presence, like children with their parents. I've noticed the same phenomenon with many of my successors. We may even stay away from and consciously or unconsciously avoid our teacher, as I did.

In my own case, within two years after receiving transmission in 1980, whenever I was around Maezumi Roshi I felt like he was sitting on my head. I felt extremely uncomfortable, practically suffocated in his presence, restrained from manifesting the power I had received.

* * *

In many spiritual paths, not only Zen, where students or followers submit to a teacher in order to receive empowerment, the teacher often expects and even demands that students submit completely, otherwise how can they be seen as serious students and worthy of receiving the Dharma? When there is intense pressure to submit, it's hard to see how abuse is not going to occur — unless the teacher is very mature and aware — because he or she is in a position of absolute power, and as we all know where there is absolute power there is the opportunity for the misuse of that power.

I think power has such negative connotations, particularly for us in the spiritual world, that we haven't looked closely enough at the issues around it. And because it is so disowned, we are not clear about how to use it. How do we manage our power if we are in denial of the power that we have? When it is disowned it comes out covertly, very often as misuse of power. If I had been seeing this earlier I might have been much more aware of how I was both using and misusing my power.

Having experienced the pain of submitting as completely as I did, I have been careful not to ask students to do certain things my teacher asked of me that I see as a misuse of his power. Nevertheless, as a teacher I too have misused my power. At various times throughout my career as a teacher, I slept with women students to whom I was sexually attracted and they to me and then lied and was not transparent with my partner and others about this deception.

I can see how I wittingly or unwittingly felt entitled to misuse my position and power for self-serving reasons and how blind I was to the damage and pain I was creating. In hindsight, either on my own or when it's been pointed out by others, I see how I ignored the way this dynamic was playing out with some female students, and the harm I inflicted on them and others in my community. Ultimately it led to my very public fall in January of 2011. Since then, acknowledging and feeling in my own heart the suffering I caused has been painful and deeply humbling.

*　　*　　*

As students we start the relationship with a teacher with a lot of positive projections. Even though we are submitting to a living teacher — a living Buddha, we say — rather than to our own understanding of the teachings, that doesn't mean that we are not still holding on to some cherished ideal of our own. We endow the teacher with all these great attributes. Some of them may be true, and a lot of them may not be. He or she, we think, is such an enlightened being, such a great Bodhisattva, so wise, and so on and so on.

Harada Roshi, one of my Dharma great-grandfathers, used to say that a Zen Master is like a blank sheet of paper the student projects on to. It's as if the teacher becomes this plain white screen for all the projections people have of what they want and hope teachers will be, and what they themselves want to get from their teacher. It seems to me that it is not only the title but also the accoutrements that go with the position — the set-up of the interview room, the robes and all that, and also the teacher's faith and trust in the Buddha-Dharma — that bring out even more projections that the teacher has got it, *is* it, some kind of pure perfect being. The more empty the teacher is, the more projections he or she gets.

The forms and practices we inherited in the Zen tradition helped build up the image of the teacher as the possessor, indeed the embodiment, of the truth. The titles 'Zen teacher,' or 'Sensei,' or even more 'Master,' or 'Roshi,' the bowing and traditional formalities of the private interview between teacher and student, where he or she is the embodiment of the lineage, everything reinforces this image. So how could what the teacher says not be the truth? I've certainly said thousands of times that I'm as human, as flawed, as bad as anybody, and still the projections have been enormous. I have held very few formal interviews since 2003 and I still see these projections. I have sat in my street clothes on a chair, I don't wear my robes, and yet people still projected this illusion of perfection on me.

*   *   *

However it is the teacher's job — and responsibility —to break this kind of illusion. At some point when the student is advanced, he or she has to be disappointed, dis-illusioned by the teacher. Not that the teacher has to try to do this; we can't help it. Sooner or later our humanness, our faults, our shadows, all our stuff, has to come out, because we are human. If we remain distant, we may keep that illusion of perfection, but then the student may not have the opportunity to become disillusioned. The closer we get the more apparent our blemishes become. From a distance everybody looks great. You get close, you see all the problems.

It's such an important part of the teacher's job, because otherwise as students we will never accept ourself as we are. We will always think 'I should be better, greater, more spiritual, more compassionate, more kind, less of an asshole, less stupid and deluded. I shouldn't be so ... human.' But the moment we can totally embrace and become the teacher — which is the point of Zen, that intimacy, to actually embody and become the teacher — we can see not only all his or her faults but we accept the teacher 100% unconditionally. At that very same moment we accept ourself 100% unconditionally. Until we can do that, it is difficult to accept ourself as we are.

In my experience, the whole point of submission and surrender in the Zen tradition, the Buddhist tradition, is that the teacher becomes real, instead of an illusion, a screen we project on. We have to go through this complete disillusionment, this complete disappointment, this complete shattering of all our notions and ideas. When we do that we become equal. This is the moment we call seeing with the same eyes, eyeball to eyeball, hearing with the same ears as the Buddhas and Masters.

And at that point gratitude and appreciation take the place of submission. We still may defer to the teacher. If the teacher says, maybe it's better you do it this way, we might go along. But not because the teacher is intrinsically superior. Maybe on a practical level he or she knows more than I do about certain things, and I have more knowledge about certain things than he or she does. But you come from that place of equality. You still appreciate the vertical, but you have no delusions or illusions about it. You're no longer blindly elevating the teacher and putting yourself down, no longer putting another head on top of your own. You have become your own final authority.

* * *

For this transformation to occur, of course it helps if the teacher too appreciates and owns this equality, which is hard to do when one is stuck on top of the mountain holding on to the feeling of power, as I was from 1980 to 2011, the years I spent really owning and empowering Mahavairochana Buddha. In retrospect I realize the reason I wasn't disturbed by all the projections was that they exactly matched my own image of myself. In other words what they saw in me was exactly what I saw in myself, it was what I projected out. So long as the students' projections matched my own, I was blind to them.

I now see why when people would ask me, 'Isn't it difficult to hold all these projections that students put on you?' I would answer, 'No.' I believed them, it was the teaching. This is the dangerous place I referred to earlier, the danger, at least for me, of getting totally identified as Mahavairochana Buddha.

Mahavairochana Buddha has only one mission, to awaken and empower Buddhas. That's all it is here to do. It doesn't care about the body and well-being of the life it embodies, except as an instrument, a vehicle. That may be what Master Dogen meant when he said to Ejo, his first successor, Never ever forget you are merely a vehicle for the Dharma. And in a way it's true, but the Dharma doesn't give a damn about the vehicle other than as a vehicle. In other words, it doesn't really care about one's personal life, family and relationships. And the self can get totally identified with it, which I did, to the point where I couldn't even see the self any more. The self was completely gone, most likely completely disowned.

So in April 2011, when Hal Stone asked me to divorce Mahavairochana Buddha and he said, 'OK, now I'd like to speak to Dennis over here,' my reaction was, 'Who?! Who's Dennis?' I mean, he was long gone, so long ago I couldn't even remember. 'Who's Dennis?' For at least three months I would sit alone, completely lost. I was completely vulnerable and raw, open and childlike. 'Who am I? Who's Dennis?' Since 1971 I had identified myself as the Buddha, since 1980 as Mahavairochana Buddha.

It seems like what happened to me in 2011 was that I fell off the high seat or the mountain top. In the five years since then I've been finding me again, the one who took all this on and went through this whole journey, this trip to get to where Mahavairochana Buddha is an aspect that I can sit in the seat of, or be, but not always, and not in my personal life on a daily basis. And I think this coming down off the mountain is an essential part of the journey. But first we have to reach the summit, and then we have to own the summit, and then we can come down from it. We can't rush any of it, it's all a journey, it's all a process.

❋   ❋   ❋

These days what I'm appreciating about the *old* masters — people like Joshu, Bodhidharma, Hyakujo and Tokusan who lived to ripe old ages — is that in my eyes they became very real, human beings. When Joshu, whose name referred to a great stone bridge, became an old man whom the young monk saw as only a broken down wooden bridge, to me that's beauty. Tokusan's unruffled response when the presumptuous young monk Seppo scolds him for coming too early to the meal, and he meekly turns around and goes back to his room — *that* is a human being. A human being, not Mahavairochana Buddha sitting on his throne. They had come down from the mountain, completely accepted their humanness, owned that they and all of us are just human beings.

I think that when we as teachers have not gone through this process and reached this level of maturity we can be blind to the student's vulnerability as well as our own. We may believe that if what we do is for the sake of the Dharma, towards awakening the student — and what isn't? — then it is justifiable. As long as we are so stuck, so strongly identified with our own clarity, perfection and power, we have a tendency to share and reinforce the very illusions that the student must eventually abandon.

* * *

We teachers need to realize that the power given to us by our students is the same power which is given back to them in order to empower them. By giving their power away, thereby making themselves very vulnerable, they are empowering us as teachers to empower them. Without giving up their attachment to their power they cannot in turn be empowered by us.

This has been known for thousands of years in the Eastern wisdom traditions. But even Eastern teachers have failed to avoid the snares inherent in this relationship, particularly after coming to the wild West and personifying these projections of power. Our responsibility as teachers in the West is to navigate this process without getting caught in its pitfalls, and to be willing to ask for guidance from a teacher or mentor we trust and respect to help us through the process.

This is one of the areas where Western psychology can offer something to the Eastern wisdom traditions, an awareness of these positive and negative bonding patterns. They are going to occur no matter what, and as teachers we need to address them in a healthy and positive way so as not to misuse our power. We have to learn how to deal with students' projections without taking them personally and becoming inflated, or hating and fearing them. We have to be willing to work with both their positive and the negative projections, and to welcome students' maturity and progress when they let them go.

This may be more difficult in the Western Dharma world than it was and still is in the East. In the Eastern male monastic setting, unlike here in the West, men and women did not practice together, nor did ordained monks and lay people. Also here in the West, in the world of therapy there exist very clear teachings about transference and countertransference, as well as about the necessity of boundaries. Therapists are taught not to get personally involved with their clients, and must observe very clear rules about this. For some types of therapy, even after a client is no longer with the therapist, the therapist must wait some years before associating with a former client.

In Zen becoming intimate and one with the teacher is an essential and crucial part of the process and the teaching. Dharma transmission is dependent on what we in Zen experience as heart-to-heart, mind-to-mind transmission, a dropping off of all boundaries. It has been my own personal experience, however, that when the teacher lacks an understanding of the dynamics of the relationships, and is him- or herself psychologically and emotionally immature, this dropping of boundaries between teacher and student can have very dangerous and damaging consequences.

I think we Zen teachers have rarely been adequately prepared to handle this relationship, particularly how to deal with the natural sexual attraction which can arise between teacher and student in this intimate setting and practice. We have tried setting up guidelines of ethical behavior, especially with regard to sexual relationships between teacher and student, usually after the fact. But this is not a matter that can be addressed simply with a set of rules and punishments, however well-intentioned and strictly enforced they may be.

It seems to me it is the responsibility of mature teachers to become educated about positive and negative bonding patterns and to educate younger successors about the harm caused by failing to understand and respect them. Just enacting rules and punishments is not enough.

If codes of conduct, not to mention the Precepts, were sufficient, sexual relationships between student and teacher would not have been so common in the short history of the Western Dharma. In my opinion, the true magnitude of this phenomenon has not really been confronted in the Buddhist world.

*　　*　　*

The forms of group practice that we followed in the West — men and women practicing and living together, teachers frequently with an open door policy for students — may have made the potential problems in the practice more apparent. However, the appropriate balance of formality, intimacy, mutual respect, and deference has always been a koan in the relationship between teacher and student.

It is very common for students and teachers to feel great love for one another. However, we need to realize that boundaries are absolutely necessary in order to deal with the love and attraction that naturally arise in such relationships, both from the student towards us as teachers and ours towards an admiring, brilliantly open student with potential to carry on the Dharma.

When a line is crossed — and I believe we always know where that line is before we've crossed it — it can become the cause of great suffering, as I can attest. Awareness that a shared love of the Dharma can be accompanied by a very strong sexual attraction, and that it is crucial to maintain appropriate boundaries and to not act it out needs to be part of the teaching here in the West.

No matter how mutual and reciprocal the emotions may seem to be, it is never simply a relationship between two equal and consenting adults, regardless of age, gender and social status. There is an inherent inequality and imbalance of power between teacher and student.

The teacher must not ignore or deny this imbalance, as I did before I recognized and experienced the confusion and pain this denial can cause. I believe that what the student is falling in love with is the Buddha innate in themselves which is embodied in the teacher, and should not be personalized or taken advantage of by the teacher. It is the teacher's responsibility to clarify this with the student.

However, it is much harder for us teachers to be clear about this when we are stuck in the experience of no-boundaries, the absolute reality where there simply are no boundaries. This is a stage on the spiritual path that is recognized and esteemed in Zen tradition, though I think its effect on the teacher-student relationship is not as well acknowledged. We may understand that in the absolute there are no boundaries, but as true as this though it is true, this understanding is still only partial. The absolute and relative are not two separate realities, there is just one reality. Coming from that perspective with wisdom and compassion, we recognize that healthy and mature boundaries are essential.

If the teacher as the one ultimately responsible crosses appropriate boundaries it can shatter the Sangha, create isolation and hell for the student, cause tremendous suffering for spouses and families involved, and bring down the teacher as well — as it did me in January of 2011.

This becoming stuck in no-boundaries may not appear to be such a problem for those who have never truly been there, especially for a very long period of time. For some teachers it is not and may never be a problem, for others like myself it was a real problem and a very tricky territory to traverse.

It is not as if I wasn't warned or given good advice and even brought to account on this very issue back in the early '90's. It seems that no set of rules or regulations could do it for me until I allowed myself to feel right down to the marrow just how much suffering and destruction I created for my wives, children, lovers, students, Sangha, friends and family as well as for myself. It took losing almost everything — wife, family, community, center, students, and reputation — and years of deep soul-searching to allow all the pain, heartbreak and suffering that I caused to really and truly hit me. And hit me it did.

*   *   *

As a teacher it is so much easier to stay in the position of power than to be vulnerable and receptive and look at ourself honestly. As a student it is much easier to shut down and shut up for fear of the consequences, to walk away from the teacher and the situation angry and resentful, talking disparagingly about the teacher's power trip. I feel if we as teachers can be mature and remain open and receptive to what the student may have to say, knowing how much courage it takes for a student to confront an authority figure in a position of power, then true communication may be possible. It takes real courage and maturity on both sides to face our fear, to let go of defensiveness and seeking to protect our position, to remain aware and respectful of the other's vulnerability.

The question is, what is necessary to transmit the teaching? I still feel that submission is an important aspect of transmission, but that it shouldn't be blind submission, just as it shouldn't be blind faith. At this point I see submission as more about being open and receptive, that real submission is based on mutual love, trust and respect between student and teacher.

However, the way submission has been understood in traditional Zen practice is deeply influenced by Japanese culture. The hierarchical structures which are so pervasive in Japanese culture are deeply embedded in Zen practice as it has come to the West. In Zen, the traditional hierarchical system involves a lot of carrots, and my understanding right now is that as long as there's a carrot, we as teachers are in an unfair position of power. We have something that somebody wants — and is willing to do whatever it takes to get. Maybe as long as there is a carrot there will be the possibility of misuse of power. In Zen, even after Dharma transmission there's still one last carrot, the final seal of approval, *Inka*.

I'm questioning any kind of carrot. I know in talking to my mentors, Drs. Hal and Sidra Stone, the creators of the Voice Dialogue method of psychotherapy, they are adamant about not offering any carrots. People can say they're Voice Dialogue therapists, but the Stones haven't empowered anybody officially. They'll say this person studied with them for ten years, twenty years, but they don't empower, they don't offer carrots.

One of the important issues in this from my standpoint as a teacher is that when we give empowerments or transmissions, part of what we're getting from it is control. So giving up those traditional forms and empowerments is also giving up control. Just before he gave the final seal of approval to Tetsugen Sensei, Maezumi Roshi said to me, "I know when I do that I'm cutting the last strings that I have for keeping control over him." He was clearly conscious that when he gave the final seal of approval he was giving up that control. "As long as I don't give it to him," he said, "I still have him on a string."

It's particularly Japanese: family, loyalty, control by the one in charge, the father or elder brother, all intertwined. Maezumi Roshi would often say, "Teacher is teacher, father is father, elder brother is elder brother always this is so. Even if you're changing your parents' diapers, they're still your parents."

We were raised on 'teacher is always teacher,' and it was up to us to always submit. As students we would always defer to him. Even after receiving the final seal of approval, if we as students had gotten together with him, we would still have deferred. We probably would have done our own thing, and still deferred to him.

If my teacher were still alive I might still be wearing Japanese clothing in daily life, and most likely not be doing Big Mind. He knew that his successors were moving away from some of the more traditional ways, and I know he knew that we were on paths different from what we had learned from him. I don't believe he was happy about it, and I don't think he could have stopped it. In his heart he knew that some of us were going in our own directions and he both liked and disliked it.

*   *   *

At this point in my journey the whole teacher-student relationship seems like such a fraught and convoluted trip, and yet I have been as much a product and a proponent of it as anyone. It is full of potential challenges, as so many incidents in the history of Buddhism in the West, including ones involving me and other Zen teachers, have made painfully apparent. And yet it may be necessary if a tradition and lineage is to be passed on.

I have seen some students who have held onto their own beliefs and ideas and refused to go this route of submission — and certainly have not been empty enough to receive Dharma transmission. There are others who have received transmission without completely submitting, and that is also problematic. In my own case, and maybe others', where we have completely submitted, that too was problematic because we became attached to submission, and at times demanded it from our most serious students, in not such a healthy way.

What to do? For me the jury is still out and the only answer I have at this time is to be as aware and mature as possible about the potential pitfalls, and to acknowledge and own our misuses of power lest we deceive ourselves and the world in the guise of doing such great and important work. In my own case it is very important for me to be open and willing to listen to students and peers, especially to their criticism, and remain accessible and willing to be vulnerable, not taking a position of self-righteousness or turning my opinion into a Dharma teaching that the student must swallow.

Since 2011, after so many years believing that submission was essential to the relation between teacher and student, and seeing how much pain the way of total submission creates for both the student and the teacher, I have been looking at the issue in a very different way.

I now see it more like longitude and latitude: the vertical and the horizontal are both essential. In the vertical we are teacher and student, in the horizontal we are fellow followers of the Way. Further, these relations can be dynamic: sometimes the teacher learns from the student. There's an openness and a flow, a heart-to-heart as well as a mind-to-mind connection. It's not static, it's always revolving and changing and dynamic.

These days I'm no longer interested in the old style of submission that I went through and also asked of my students for decades. I don't think submission can work anymore in the old 'traditional Japanese' way here in the West. I see that there needs to be a heart-to-heart connection based on love, trust and respect, an openness to one another with clear and appropriate boundaries set by the teacher, honoring position place and time as well as appropriate amount of giving and receiving. It means that we teachers also have to be open to students by being respectful, caring and responsible, and always aware of their vulnerability, as well as our own.

Understanding the complexity of the student-teacher relationship, it is our responsibility as teachers to protect the integrity of the relationship. Most students are not entering the situation with years of wisdom and maturity that we as teachers should have. As new and young teachers we need to be aware of the power imbalance inherent in the relationship, and the potential misuse of our position of power. And as mature teachers we also need to teach prospective teachers as much as possible about the pitfalls along the way, especially until they grow more mature and hopefully wiser.

LIVING ZEN

3

How I Came to Zen

Many people embark on the path of a spiritual practice in response to a profound existential question or crisis. When I went out to the Mohave Desert on a February day back in 1971 I was not aware of searching for anything deeper than to understand how I could have screwed up my life so completely at such an early age.

I had gone out there on a whim because I was having some difficulty with my girlfriend and needed to get away. I called in sick to the school where I had been teaching in Long Beach California. I was there with my best friend Kurt Goerwitz and his girlfriend from Santa Barbara.

While they ventured off into the desert I climbed a small mountain where I had a great 360^0 view and sat down cross-legged contemplating my life. At the age of twenty-six I had already been divorced a couple of years earlier and was in a new relationship facing the same old problems, feeling trapped and criticized by my new partner as I had felt previously by my wife. Sitting there in Jaw Bones Canyon in the middle of the Mohave Desert I began to ask the question, "Where is home?"

What happened at that moment was absolutely mind-blowing, unlike anything I had ever experienced before. My self was dropped off and I became one with the entire cosmos, God, the Creator and all creations, all things. I had returned home, and realized that I had never left it, that wherever I was, I was always home. Everything finally made sense, life was simple and uncomplicated and I was absolutely liberated and at peace. I had realized that I was awake, the Way. I was God, the Creator. All creations, animate as well as inanimate, were me.

What appeared spontaneously was a desire to further clarify the

Way and at the same time to assist others in the process of awakening. This initial experience was so profoundly life-transforming that I felt compelled to share it with anyone interested in listening. It was like reading the greatest book or seeing the best movie ever made and just wanting to share it with everyone.

My experience could have been related to the sudden death of my father in June of 1968 when he was only fifty-eight years old, just a week after I turned twenty-four. My dad tended to do things in an extreme way. He worked what my family called two weeks in one, meaning the he worked a seventy-two hour week as a tool and die maker. He had recently gotten back into running several miles before work every morning as well as calisthenics and spending what time off he had playing three-wall handball. It seemed he was always competing with me to be in the best shape. I had just a year before quit working out for a spot on the U.S. Olympic water polo team. I'd had a good relationship with him but since getting married in '66 it had become a little strained. I know he was very proud of my receiving my Master's Degree from the University of Southern California one week earlier. My younger sister had been married just a few months and my dad died the day before her twenty-first birthday. This may have triggered in me some unconscious seeking for the meaning of life and death, but unconscious it was.

My buddy Kurt said it sounded like I had had a Zen experience, that I sounded like the Zen Masters he had studied while earning his Doctorate in Psychology at UCSB. I had only heard the word Zen spoken once before, about four or five months earlier, by a good friend named Fred Ancheta, now better known as Jitsudo Roshi, whom I had known since junior high school.

From then on I began to study everything I could get my hands on about Zen, Buddhism, Christian and Jewish mysticism as well as Western psychology. I became what I had never been before, an avid reader, devouring everything in print on these subjects as well as sitting zazen three times a day or even more.

That week I quit my job as well as my relationship. I began a practice of regular zazen, reading and getting away from people as much as possible. Every weekend I would drive with my two friends deep into the mountains east of Santa Barbara to Big and Little Calienta Hot Springs, along with some of the other young and beautiful hippies of our generation.

After the school year was up I sold or gave away all my belongings and headed off to the Pacific Northwest and Canada with just a backpack, a sleeping bag and a change of clothing. I was known as Sebastian because the only shirt I wore besides my t-shirts was an old army shirt that had the name Sebastian sewn above the pocket. It was easier to go by that name than to explain why I wasn't Sebastian. There are still folks out there in the world who know me as Sebastian.

It was truly a great year, one of the happiest of my life. I was free and had few or no responsibilities or possessions. I ended up hiking over a glacier fifty miles into the back country in Glacier National Park and meeting up with a grizzly bear the night after a woman had been mauled to death at the very same campground. It was there in June of 1971 at a site called Fifty Mountain Peak, where you could actually look down on fifty mountain peaks, that I realized I was destined to be a Zen Master and to assist others in waking up. It seemed preposterous to me at that moment for I had not met a teacher nor had any real training. I was just a young former school teacher and lifeguard from Long Beach California.

After three or four months of backpacking and hitchhiking I lived as the caretaker of a beautiful piece of property near San Luis Obispo up in the Los Padres National Forest. It had a rustic little cabin built by a wonderful musician from UCSB, with three streams merging together just behind it. I lived there until June of '72, alone for nine of the ten months I was there, and without transportation for the first several months. It was five miles to the closest neighbor and the local town of Santa Margarita. I didn't see another person for some three months until one day a cowboy rode up on his horse and asked me if I'd seen any stray "dogies" (cattle) around, to which I answered no I hadn't. He then tipped his hat and rode off.

While living at the cabin I sat zazen for three to four hours a day, chopped wood (the only heating was a fireplace) and carried two buckets of water a day from the stream. One was for drinking, the second for washing up with Dr. Bronner's biodegradable soap when it got too cold to bathe in the pond. Every evening I would cook a pot of brown rice on a Coleman camping stove and add whatever else I had, potatoes or canned vegetables, some brewer's yeast and lecithin powder for good measure. That was my breakfast and lunch for the next day as well. I would open a bottle of wine every few days and sip it with dinner as I wrote letters, and my philosophy of life and Zen.

That Christmas I was given a German Shepherd dog that had been mistreated. Her favorite pastime was chasing cows, and I believe the poor dog was eventually shot by one of the cowboys who had warned me to not let her do that. It was next to impossible to stop her without tying her up all the time, which I was not about to do. So she met her fate at the hands of a rifleman with good aim.

I started a sitting group with about twenty people who would come out to the cabin twice a week. We would sit in zazen and then I would read aloud a chapter from Suzuki Roshi's book *Zen Mind Beginner's Mind*. We practiced massage, astrology, and yoga as well as zazen together. It was during one of my solitary sittings at the cabin in March of '72 that I realized I am the Buddha and that I needed to submit myself to a Buddha who was an authentic master in a genuine lineage tracing its roots all the way back to Shakyamuni Buddha.

I emphasize here that the realization was not that I was 'a' Buddha; it was that I was THE Buddha. That is what made it both so profound and so unbelievable. This is why I needed to find a living Buddha/Patriarch to work on my ego which I felt had become so inflated from all these profound realizations of who I was.

The very next day a black Cadillac drove up and out stepped an elderly gentleman dressed all in black, carrying black meditation cushions. His name was Earl Eddy, and he told me it was time for me to meet a true Zen Master, Koryu Roshi, and his successor Maezumi Sensei, who was himself about to become a Zen Master.

Within three days I had hopped a railway flatcar down to LA

and was face to face with Maezumi Sensei at the Zen Center of Los Angeles. My first impression was not good. I thought he was cold and distant.

The retreat was difficult for me, I was having a tremendous amount of leg pain. Because I was young and strong, able to bench-press nearly four hundred pounds at the time, I was assigned to assist Maezumi Sensei moving large boulders in a couple of rock gardens he was creating. He would tell me where to place the boulder and I would struggle to maneuver it into exactly the right place. He would step back, meditate on it for a while and then say No, I want it over there. I'd manage to get into place and he'd step back and ponder it for a while, only to say he liked it better where it was before.

This went on over and over again, as I became increasingly exasperated. At that time, I did not know the story of Milarepa and the trials he endured under his teacher Marpa, but when I heard it, it certainly sounded familiar. By the fourth day I was ready to quit. My legs were killing me and I felt frustrated with the practice. I had been in a much more serene and peaceful place up at my cabin than I was in this seven-day retreat in the heart of Los Angeles.

We were out working in the garden when I told Maezumi Sensei I was going to quit that day. His reply shocked me, and touched my heart. He said to me three times, "I don't want you to go." No one had ever said something like that to me before. It wasn't, You shouldn't go, or you can't go; it was *I don't want you to go.* That truly moved me.

I had told him that what we were practicing there at ZCLA was not Zen. "All the bowing and rituals are not true Zen!" "What is Zen?" he demanded. "Just *this*!" I answered, ramming the spade I was holding into the ground. Then he asked me where I had studied and with whom. With no one, I said, I am living deep in the mountains in a small cabin, sitting about four hours a day, chopping wood and carrying water, reading D.T. Suzuki and Alan Watts. "Alan Watts!" he shouted, "he is not Zen!"

Then he said something that went straight into my heart like a dagger: "You are the most arrogant young man I have ever met."

Then he asked me to come up to his room after lunch to talk about it all before leaving.

By the time lunch was over some hours later I had already decided not to leave the retreat. I was glad that I stayed and when I returned to my mountain cabin that week I sat with our conversation and decided he was absolutely right, that I was very arrogant. I wrote him a letter saying he was right and asked him what I should do now. He wrote back, "Nose is vertical, eyes are horizontal, mountains are high, valleys are low, sun rises in the East and sets in the West. Continue to do exactly what you have been doing, living alone in the mountains and sitting zazen several hours a day."

Five months later, in August of 1972, I moved down to Los Angeles and Maezumi Roshi. He had received the final seal of approval from Koryu Roshi during that same retreat where I had first met him, a year after receiving it from Yasutani Roshi, but refused to use the title Roshi until finishing koans and study with Koryu Roshi. He allowed me to live in my Dodge van in the ZCLA parking lot for a few weeks until I found an apartment. In September I moved in across the street from the Center and began formal Zen practice.

4

Some Things I Have Learned

Looking back with what I like to call 40/40 hindsight at the more than forty years since I made the conscious decision to enter formal Zen practice with my Zen Master Maezumi Roshi, I am often asked what I have received and learned in all this time. What I have discovered is how to be happy and at peace, to face whatever arises in my life with joy and stability. There is a serenity as well as liberation from being confused and dissatisfied with life. A strong faith that everything that happens, happens just perfectly and it is all a teaching. Some teachings are more painful than others, but it is all teaching, it's all Dharma: To appreciate this life and realize that all is impermanent, to own and embody all parts of myself, the bad as well as the good, the failures as well as the successes. To live most of the time from the Apex, with integrity and transparency in my relationships with loved ones and others, and most importantly with myself.

I could say I have gained absolutely nothing from practicing Zen — and yet it feels like I have gained everything. It has been a wonderful but difficult journey to settle and find happiness, peace and freedom with myself. I say nothing is gained because from the beginning nothing was missing. Anything gained would eventually be lost because it is extra.

In the past few years, as some of the clouds of great loss and heartbreak have parted, a deeper faith and happiness has been revealed. Some of my most painful learning has come from realizing the suffering my infidelity has caused my wives, children, family, loved ones and students. I wish that I had learned a long time ago the damage that unfaithfulness and lying create. Seeing the deep pain and suffering I have caused I realize how essential it is for me to live with integrity and transparency. It took many years and a couple of falls for me to truly get it, but get it I did.

I've also learned how to live with vulnerability, with an open heart easily moved and touched by others and the pain and suffering we all face on our journey. Of course I have known for decades that we are all one and yet each of us is unique, and that it is the differences that make each individual, each culture, each religion and each nation unique. But it is only in these last few years that I have come to realize how much I actually love and appreciate each person's differences, regardless of whether they think or act like me. Imagine a world where we could all come from oneness and yet love and appreciate our differences rather than fearing and hating them!

There is an old Zen saying that first a mountain is a mountain, then after awakening a mountain is no longer a mountain, then once again a mountain is just a mountain. That's what it has been like for me. Living life as a human being was once just living life as a human being, then it no longer was as I had known it, and now living life as a human being is just that, and yet it's not the same as before. There is much more vulnerability and awareness of life's impermanence and our human condition, the suffering of all beings and fragility of life. There is deep desire to be kinder and more loving to all those I come into contact with, to be more present and see their humanity and vulnerability. The Buddhist Precepts which I received from Maezumi Roshi more than four decades ago, and have given to literally hundreds of people myself, are not a set of rules or commandments; not living them is just too painful and hurtful.

I realize that one of my big mistakes was thinking I needed to embody the extremes — good and evil, right and wrong, life and death, saint and sinner, enlightened and deluded, etc. What I did not understand was that it is one thing to own and transcend these extremes, it is another to live them out. I felt that I had a Double-O license to be both great and entitled, heroically selfless and inflated and self-centered.

What I didn't realize was that whatever extreme we own and

embody, its opposite can still come out covertly. I was embodying the Zen Master, a Dharma heir and Patriarch in the 81st generation of the lineage descending directly from the historical Buddha, but I had no sense of its opposite, and how that was playing itself out. Because I was so identified with the good I was doing, I overlooked and ignored the bad.

Because I felt I was giving my whole life to the Dharma, I sometimes felt entitled to be self-centered and to gratify my ego. Identified as I was with being the Zen Master and an 81st Patriarch, I sometimes took for granted the trust and love offered to me in that position, without fully appreciating the vulnerability of those entrusting me with their heart and soul. These days it makes me sad to think of the pain I caused those who loved and respected me. For this I am truly sorry, and I write with the hope that sharing my mistakes will be helpful to others on the Path.

Maezumi Roshi used to call me 'the wild one' because at times I was quite rebellious and crazy. He said I was very green and immature, and he was right. It has taken me years to grow up and mature. I realize I haven't always been a good role model, I have made mistakes, let people down, badly disappointed them. So I am constantly working on myself and refining my life to be in accord with the Way. It is an endless process. Deeply rooted patterns are a bitch. It is like Tokusan's Thirty Blows — thirty blows if you answer, thirty blows if you don't. This is life: whatever you do, you will receive thirty blows.

It seems we must die over and over again to who we are in order to be reborn time and time again. I was not living the wisdom that I already knew and even taught. The power that we have been blessed with is a gift that flows through us directly from the Source, it does not belong to us. When others entrust us with power, we should not misuse it, for power misused becomes abusive. When others entrust us with power we have the potential to awaken and to heal them; when this power is misused we lose, and do not deserve, their trust.

Even the subtle misuse of power, which we may often be unaware of, is abusive. When we are not fully awakened to the power bestowed upon us by another through title and position, we tend to become arrogant. That sense of superiority itself is a misuse of power because it separates us from others. So how do we live the teachings of the Buddha with integrity, without being self-righteous about it? That's not so easy.

When I first began studying Zen, we all tried to be Japanese, Tibetan, or something other than who and what we were. I've learned not to get caught up in trying to be something I'm not in order to be more 'authentic.' In the end it just doesn't work. As Westerners we need to find Western ways to train and Western forms, we need to be comfortable in our own skin. The same is true for trying to be another person, whoever it may be, because I can never be another as well as they can be themselves and they can never be me better than I can. So rather than competing with others, I am just myself. That also means seeing myself clearly, owning my shadows as much as possible, and not being too critical of others, for most likely whatever I criticize in others is a shadow of mine. Only I don't see it; most likely everyone else does.

I believe we can learn from our mistakes and possibly only from them. At least I haven't learned nearly as much from 'being right' as I have from seeing where I've been wrong. It seems it's the falls that really bring us the most necessary growth and the greatest humility. I see that with the heartaches in life, the loss of name and reputation, and even the aging process and the body failing us. It seems that it is pain that teaches us the deepest lessons.

These days I even find myself genuinely appreciating the sixty-six Zen teachers who signed a letter asking me to stop teaching Zen for a period of time in order to help me learn my lessons. Without their ruthless compassion, and compassion it was, I don't believe I would be as happy and free as I am today and in such a beautiful and thankful place in my life.

It is my intention to never stop learning, and never stop being a student. Even with the title 'Roshi' I am forever a student and a beginner. As Suzuki Roshi said, a Zen mind is a beginner's mind. How to maintain this mind? A beginner's mind is open, flexible and fresh, coming from not knowing; an ignorant mind is closed, inflexible and knowing.

5

Being OK with What Is

It has taken me forty-five years of Zen practice and a great deal of inner searching and suffering to be at a place where I can really say from the bottom of my heart that being OK or not OK is OK.

In 1971, soon after Thomas A. Harris published his book "I'm OK, You're OK," I had the good fortune to attend a weekend course with him at UCLA. Then in 1973, I heard Yamada Koun Roshi give a talk at ZCLA and say that what Zen is and where it differs from Mr. Harris is that in Zen you are not OK, I am not OK, but that is OK. Some years later, in 1981, while I was visiting him at his home in Kamakura Japan he said privately to me that it wasn't until he reached the age of seventy that he was free from concern about what others thought or said about him.

Now that I am past seventy myself, I feel that I am finally free to let people say and think whatever they choose and to be who and what they are. I don't need to fix them or change them, nor to fix or change myself to suit them. I can just allow myself to be who I am.

Of course I am still continuously studying and refining myself, coming from the place of being OK as I am, and yet knowing I need to work on my issues and shadows. I also continue to guide and work with others, coming from that place where they are OK and yet not, and I am not OK, and that is OK. It is such a peaceful and free place to be, and feels like reaping the benefits of a lifetime of practice.

Dogen Zenji said, "A Zen master's life is one continuous mistake." Now I really see the wisdom of this. He is not putting himself down. On the contrary, he is truly appreciating his life, with all its ups and downs, trials and tribulations, successes and failures. We make one mistake after another and no matter how hard we try we will always make mistakes, it is unavoidable.

Maybe we learn only from our mistakes and life is just one chance to learn after another. As the great Zen Master Kodo Sawaki said, to win is to lose and in Zen to lose everything is to win. Maybe to lose it all is to find our humanity, happiness and freedom.

I realized decades ago that the second phase of our koan practice, after realizing the oneness of life and all things, is to recognize their subtle differences. However it only recently struck me that this teaching really is to appreciate and even love these differences. We are all looking for agreement and want our partners, loved ones, friends and family to think like us and to believe as we do, but what does it require to truly appreciate others' differences?

What would it take to truly love and appreciate other countries and cultures, religions and creeds, different views and beliefs, understandings and ways of being? To come from seeing the oneness and yet appreciate the differences? This world would truly be transformed.

6

My Practice These Days

These past five plus years I've been very much like a person emptying his house — every appliance, every piece of furniture and clothing — out on the front lawn. Having put everything out, now I can choose what to bring back in, what needs to be reupholstered or repaired before I'll keep it, and what new items I need to replace the old ones that aren't working for me any more.

Of all the teachings and tradition I've learned and received over the past forty-five years, one part of my practice that has come back into my life in quite a different form than it had in the past is my way of sitting for meditation. For a while I sat much less than I had for the first forty years and even gave up zazen on a daily basis, only to find that it hadn't given up on me. Since then, sitting and devotion have come back into my life, and they are giving me greater joy and fulfillment than ever.

Until recently I sat cross-legged in a lotus posture with my back straight and unsupported. These days my posture is entirely different, and I am loving sitting more than ever. I sit completely relaxed and comfortable, usually on a chair, my legs often not crossed, feet on the floor, resting my back against the back of the chair, upright but not stiff or rigid in any way.

I begin the sitting with ten very slow deep breaths, expelling all the air through my mouth with lips narrowly puckered, breathing in through my nose. I continue to count these slow breaths from one to ten repeatedly with mouth closed, through the nostrils. Then I drop the counting and just sit without preference or judgements.

Maybe because I am aging I find that with my back supported and my legs not crossed in a lotus posture, I can completely relax and have no pain anywhere in my body. I used to sit forty to sixty minutes at a time without pain; these days I often sit two to four hours in one go without pain.

I sit with no judgment about my sitting, no preference for being awake over being asleep, attentive over inattentive, aware over unaware — without any goal or objective, aim or purpose. I just sit upright, comfortable, relaxed and natural. The key is I give myself complete permission to just sit without judging my sitting in any way.

I usually sit as the one coming from what I call non-preference, non-judgement, non-thinking, non-seeking, beyond thinking or not thinking, etc. There is no observer, no witness, only a deep and complete relaxation. It is bliss and joyful samadhi. It is self-empowering samadhi, dropped off dropped off. In this sitting there is an absence of self. At times there is no one present to be aware or not aware, awake or not awake, no coming or going, knowing or not knowing, thinking or not thinking, beyond all.

In this samadhi there is a thin, almost indistinguishable line between alive or dead, breath and no breath, conscious or unconscious. It is absolutely blissful and silk-like. The entire body is relaxed, from head to toes, right down to the cellular level. All stress and tension in body and mind are completely released. It is like being dead while still alive, and this samadhi gets carried over into daily life as a pure childlike happiness I have never experienced before. There is real joy and pleasure in serving and being present for others.

These days I often include a highly personal devotional practice, offering my prayers and my sitting to others and bowing down in reverence, inviting or asking for guidance and assistance from the Buddhas and Bodhisattvas. It's my own version of Atonement and Repentance. Realizing that as a self I am just a speck in the cosmos — vulnerable, fragile and limited like everyone and everything else — I invite a power greater than myself to enter. At other times I just sit without a goal or aim. Or I surrender and relinquish my own will to that which is greater than my ego-centered self, allowing that energy in.

As I age I have become more aware of my own limitations and

arrogance in thinking I can do it all myself. I have had to learn — the hard way — about facing and owning the fact that I am truly powerless. It's Tokusan's Thirty Blows. No matter what we do we're going to get beaten, life will beat us and we're going to lose, through sickness old age and finally death.

At this point in my life I have no fear of death and just live moment to moment, having few desires and appreciating this life with all its ups and downs, gains and losses. Eventually I will lose all those I love and all I am attached to. I have to relinquish completely, realizing that I can't always get it right nor cling to what I have. I just surrender moment after moment. Continuous relinquishment, that is my practice these days.

7

Having Nothing to Teach

And yet, even as I speak, Subhuti, I must take back my words as soon as they are uttered, for there are no Buddhas and there are no teachings.

—The Buddha, *The Diamond Sutra*

After more than forty years of sharing the Dharma, and all the words that I have spoken, written and recorded, when I'm asked what my teaching is these days, I feel I must say that I have nothing to teach, that is my teaching. I have attained nothing, for who is there that would attain it, and what is it that was lacking from the beginning and needed to be attained?

The wisdom we wish to attain is already innate within each of us, what we seek we already have. There is no teaching, no enlightenment and no enlightened person. Though we may try to deny or reject it, what we eventually realize after years of practice, ups and downs, successes and failures, is that we are all just human beings. We have two sides to our nature, the human and the being. The human is just human, with all our imperfections and desires, gains and losses; the being is already complete, perfect and whole and there is nothing missing or extra.

As the Buddha says in the *Diamond Sutra*:

"Tell me Subhuti, does a Buddha say to himself, 'I have obtained Perfect Enlightenment.'?"

"No, lord. There is no such thing as Perfect Enlightenment to obtain. If a Perfectly Enlightened Buddha were to say to himself, 'I am enlightened' he would be admitting there is an individual person, a separate self and personality, and would therefore not be a Perfectly Enlightened Buddha."

One thing I have realized is that there is no particular universal meaning to life. It is nothing other than what we bring to it by giving and serving others. When Master Rinzai was asked, "What is the meaning of Bodhidharma coming from the West?" his answer was, "If he had had a reason, he could not even have saved himself!"

Our life unfolds continuously and is always a mystery, if it were other it would be hell. What we have is just our karma and that is our Dharma, both our teaching for ourself and what we can share with others.

What all enlightened beings have realized is just this: there is nothing to be attained and this is the Absolute Truth. We want to believe there is a Way, and if we only can attain it we will be saved, or free. The realization is that there is no Way, no way out, no escape, no liberation and no one to be liberated. There is just this life and our pain and suffering.

We are the Way and there is no other Way. We can only stop fighting and resisting pain and suffering, and be one with it. There is no one and no thing we can lean or depend on that will make it all OK; it is just OK as it is. There is no nirvana apart from samsara, no enlightenment apart from delusion.

Again, in the *Diamond Sutra*, the venerable Subhuti speaks of himself (interestingly, in the third person):

> "Yet I do not say to myself that I am so [that I have obtained Perfect Enlightenment], for if I ever thought of myself as such then it would not be true that I escaped ego delusion. I know that in truth there is no Subhuti and therefore Subhuti abides nowhere, that he neither knows nor does he not know bliss, and that he is neither free from nor enslaved by his passions."

There is no Buddha, no enlightened beings, no Dharma and no Way. The world is neither good nor evil, sane nor insane, neither holy nor unholy, form nor formless. It is nothing and yet is just as it is. Nothing matters and yet everything matters, there is no cause and effect and yet there is only cause and effect. There is no karma and yet there is no escape from karma. Awakening is not freedom from karma; rather, it is not ignoring karma, being one with our karma.

There are no enlightened people and yet everyone is intrinsically enlightened. The difference between an enlightened person and a so-called unenlightened person is that the unenlightened thinks there is a difference and the enlightened knows there is no difference. Those who speak often do not know and those who know often do not speak. The wise know they are but fools and fools think that they are wise. The deluded think that they are enlightened and the enlightened know that they are deluded.

In the Diamond Sutra the Buddha says, "It cannot be said that anything is attainable."

> Then Subhuti asks, "World-Honored One, in the attainment of the consummation of incomparable enlightenment did Buddha make no acquisition whatsoever?"
> Buddha replies: "Just so, Subhuti. Through the consummation of incomparable enlightenment I acquired not even the least thing; wherefore it is called 'consummation of incomparable enlightenment.'"

The question often arises, how do we know when we have reached enlightenment? We know when we have realized without a shadow of a doubt that there is no enlightenment to be attained and all seeking has come to an end. When it is clear that there is absolutely nothing missing or lacking, nothing to be attained and no one to attain such a thing as enlightenment, that there is no above or below, for there is no other. It is not a matter of knowing and not knowing. Knowing is delusion and not knowing can manifest as irresponsible ignorance. The Way is beyond knowing and not knowing.

When the great Chinese Master Joshu was asked what was his teaching, he said, "When I teach, I go directly to the core of the matter," and when asked what is the core of the matter he answered it is "right in front of the eyes," "the oak tree in the front garden," "the leg of the chair," "the scorched kettle."

For me too, the teaching is right in front of our eyes: it is a beautiful sunset, the blue sea and the green mountains. It is chopping wood and carrying water or changing the baby's diaper and emptying the garbage. It is paying the bills on time, going to work or making your flight. It embraces and yet is beyond the personal and impersonal, relative and absolute, the worldly and the spiritual.

These days I have a deep appreciation for the ancient ancestors like Bodhidharma and the great Chinese Zen Masters like the Sixth Patriarch, Tokusan, Hyakujo and Joshu, for whom the teaching is beyond words and letters, beyond and yet including all opposites such as thinking and not thinking, seeking and not seeking, doing and not doing. It is beyond yet embraces the personal and impersonal, form and emptiness, right and wrong, good and bad, the relational and the non-relational.

I feel a strong sense of kinship with the line of radical Zen Masters of China whose teachings were innovative, non-conformist, eccentric and at times rebellious, challenging tradition, not politically correct nor shaped by a desire to fit into society's norms. Being true to their lineage means not marginalizing the profundity of Zen in order to have it fit ideas of what is right or wrong, but rather upholding the integrity of true Zen, where realization is the backbone of Zen, not notions of what will be accepted by our society and culture.

Being true to the lineage also means distinguishing the bones from the essence of the tradition. Particularly for those of us in the West, if it is really going to take root here, it is our responsibility as stewards of this Dharma that has been transmitted generation after generation to realize Bodhidharma's profound meaning which is, in his own words, beyond words and letters.

We must be able to freely and confidently answer such questions as, "Why did Bodhidharma come from the West?" and, "Why has the Western barbarian no beard?" If we think it's because he either had or didn't have a beard, we are gravely mistaken.

Of course these koans must be presented before a teacher who has thoroughly penetrated them. Without this dynamic exchange, true Zen will die out. It will become just another practice of meditation and spirituality only to feel good.

Emperor Wu asked Bodhidharma who he was, but missed the opportunity to grasp the meaning of his answer. How do we understand Bodhidharma's "I know not"? His not-knowing is the not-knowing of someone who has searched for the meaning of life and death to the very depths of the sea and the far corners of the universe, and has realized without a shadow of a doubt the meaning of Bodhidharma coming from the West. Only Bodhidharma can know his true meaning. When we have become one with this old barbarian and sat as he did for years, then possibly we may go beyond the dual and the non-dual as well.

The point here is have we, like Emperor Wu, missed our window of opportunity to truly meet the old barbarian? If we have had the opportunity and did not manage to swallow him in a single gulp, we may be still be holding on to our notions and deeply held beliefs of being right or our fear of being wrong. Bodhidharma will never come back, and if we want to get to the Truth, we must swallow our pride, cross the great river and chase after him. If there is anything left of our pride, of our ideas of right and wrong, we will not see him face-to-face ever again.

We are in a time where many people teaching spirituality have very little to no experience of true practice and of profound realization. Many want to make a living teaching meditation but haven't gone through serious practice themselves. They may have had some opening or mystical experience, but is it of the same caliber and depth that the old masters are speaking about?

As Dogen Zenji wrote, enlightenment embraces training. The history of Zen records countless examples of those who had to go through tremendous hardship in order to attain true realization, and years of practice to actualize it in their daily lives. It is Shakyamuni Buddha's teaching that training encompasses enlightenment. There is no enlightenment apart from training. Practice is enlightenment, enlightenment is practice.

In working with students I regard koans and Big Mind as complementary practices. They may have an opening, even advance in their practice. However, without a regular sitting practice it may be difficult for them to integrate any realization into their daily lives.

How does training imply enlightenment? Training is realization and only through training are we able to manifest our true nature in everyday life. It is a very subtle point, impossible to grasp fully unless one has had direct experience of it. It reveals that whatever we do from morning until night is no other than the manifestation of our true nature.

> The great Master Yakusan was asked by his attendant, "Sir the monks are complaining that you have not given a teaching for quite some time. Would your Reverence please agree to give us a teaching?"
>
> The old Master agreed and had the attendant monk gather the students in the Dharma Hall. Yakusan ascended the high seat, sat there for some time without saying a word,. and then descended and returned to his room.
>
> The attendant monk chasing after him said, "Master, you agreed to give a teaching, but you said nothing!"
>
> The Master said, "There are Sutra Teachers to teach the Sutras and Commentary Teachers to teach the commentaries, why do you bother this old Zen monk?"

On the other hand, there are people who, after having had some glimpse of enlightenment, prematurely conclude that since enlightenment is nothing but one's life, after realization everything can be called practice and it no longer matters how much they practice meditation. What may originally have been a genuine realization becomes a big delusion and simply a way to justify oneself. Without real guidance, it is very easy to fall into one of these traps.

8

Gratitude for the Old Masters

Nowadays we have more information at our fingertips than ever before, but some learning just can't be rushed. What takes time simply takes time. We can pass a koan, see a koan, suddenly — the realization takes no time. To clarify, to deepen, to embody and actually live the koan, that takes time.

I have been at this a long time now, and I have never appreciated these old masters and their koans as much as I have in these past few years. I needed to live life, experience my rises and falls, to appreciate the sacrifices and the steadfastness of these old guys firsthand, what it really took to pass on the great teachings we benefit from today.

We tend to idealize these old masters and turn their lives into legends that seem so remote and unattainable. We are amazed at the thought of a young monk face to face with someone like Master Tokusan, receiving thirty blows from his stick. But how do we receive these blows? Do we resist, make him wrong? Do we run or do we bow deeply? How do we face our teacher and his blows? We glorify the old koans but how do we live them day to day?

Consider this story from Master Tokusan's later years, the koan called "Old Tokusan Carries His Bowls:"

> One day when the lunch was late Tokusan came down to the dining room carrying his bowls. Seppo, who was in charge of cooking, said, "Old Master, the bell has not yet rung nor the drum sounded. Where are you going with your bowls?" Tokusan turned around at once and meekly walked back to his room.
>
> Seppo told this incident to Ganto, who remarked, "Great Master though he is, Tokusan has not yet grasped the last word of Zen."
>
> Hearing of this, Tokusan sent his attendant to summon Ganto and then asked him, "Don't you approve of this old monk?" Ganto

whispered his intention. Tokusan remained silent.

Sure enough, the next day, when Tokusan ascended the rostrum, his talk was quite different from usual. Ganto, rubbing his hands together, laughed and said, "Wonderful! How happy I am that our old Master has realized the last word of Zen. From now on nobody in the whole world can ever make light of him."

How do we appreciate this old Tokusan when he meekly turns around and goes back to his room after being chastised by young Seppo, the cook? Without living that humiliation ourselves can we appreciate where Tokusan was coming from and how he had changed since his days of beating his monks?

Can we appreciate where Seppo was coming from when he felt he had truly bested his old master once and for all, unless we own and acknowledge that we ourselves were that proud and arrogant, wanting to beat our old teacher in our own competitive way?

Can we really appreciate what Ganto was up to when he said if the old man had only realized the last word of Zen no one could have made light of him, if we haven't played that game our self with fellow students and our own teacher? Can we really appreciate what Ganto whispered without having been that intimate with our own Master and whispered the same thing to him or her?

Appreciation takes time and living. We all know how difficult it is for young people to appreciate this life and their youth. We have that harsh saying, "Youth is wasted on the young." We can have clarity when we are young, but I wonder if we can truly appreciate what these old masters gave up and endured before we ourselves have gone through life. I had to lose it all and drop it all, to move far away from the whole Zen trip and return years later, to appreciate it as I do now. Nowadays when I read or tell these old koans and stories I cry in deep gratitude knowing intimately what they had to go through.

This is not just ancient history. I remember when a group of us including Maezumi Roshi were having tea with Uchiyama Roshi and he told us how he had been thrown out first by his peer group of successors in the lineage of Kodo Sawaki, then by the Soto Zen School, then by the whole Buddhist community for being involved in ecumenical dialogues with Christians. "Now," he said, ripping open his kimono and showing us his bare chest, "all I have left is, JUST THIS!" How can we truly appreciate what it must have been like for such a devoted Buddhist as he was, to go through such public humiliation?

How must Maezumi Roshi have felt at the very end of his life, to say, "I realize I have become the last barrier for my successors to transmit the Buddha-Dharma in the West"? What a humbling thought, after giving more than forty years to propagating the Dharma. It is these kinds of rises and falls, successes and failures, that go into ripening and leveling of one's ego.

Another old Zen story that has really resonated with me quite recently is of the hermit, Master Ryokan, who came home one night after a thief had broken into his little hut only to find nothing to steal. The story goes that Ryokan caught up with the thief and said to him, "You have come a long way to visit me, and you should not return empty-handed. Please take my clothes as a gift." Then sitting naked, looking up at the beautiful full moon hiding behind some clouds, Ryokan composed this poem:

> The thief left it behind:
> the moon
> at my window.

It is so inspiring for me these days to reflect and speak about these old masters, considering what they had to go through to be as ripe and mature as a Joshu, a Tokusan or a Bodhidharma. You don't become like that without living and experiencing real life and suffering. Climbing to the top of the mountain and descending, sometimes even falling all the way to the bottom, maybe even a few times. Ascending and descending, gaining and losing, winning and failing.

We all reach moments when we are ready to die or give up, how do we handle these moments? Do we kill ourselves or do we completely surrender and go on renewed and freshly inspired to be reborn after the death of the self? Can we lose everything — loved ones, family, friends, name, reputation, position, health — and yet continue to grow and expand, to re-inspire ourselves for the sake of the Dharma to carry on and offer the teachings?

Uchiyama Roshi's teacher Kodo Sawaki Roshi said, 'To win is to lose, to lose is to win, to lose all is to win all.' True Zen has always been about first ascending then descending the mountain, not remaining on top. On top we are completely deluded in our enlightenment. Our practice is to be like a lotus in muddy water, a phoenix rising from the ashes. This is what we call "the hazy moon of enlightenment."

Few in our day and age can appreciate this truth. We all want to hold on to hope, to the notion that somehow there is an escape from this life of suffering. This is the view one hears from many spiritual teachers who do not have very deep realizations but are popular because they hold out hope for a way out through some special practice or other, avoiding the truth that there really is no place to go and nothing to get. However, to truly get that takes years of dedicated practice, of seeking to realize or grasp the Un-graspable; it doesn't come from halfhearted effort and lack of real discipline.

What so many of us in this age of the spiritual supermarket don't understand is that our practice is to lose it all. Before great enlightenment our realizations are like the openings of a camera lens, one moment a glimpse, the next the lens closes and we lose that clarity. So we hold on to our glimpses for dear life.

With great awakening the lens does not close again. We live that realization, integrating it into every aspect of our life. All doubt in who we are is gone forever. But this is where we can get stuck even more than ever before, where, as some great masters like Dogen Zenji have said, enlightenment is delusion.

In his *Fukanzazengi*, Dogen Zenji writes:

> The Way is basically perfect and all-pervading. How could it be contingent upon practice and realization? The Dharma vehicle is free and untrammeled. What need is there for man's concentrated effort? Indeed, the whole body is far beyond the world's dust. Who could believe in a means to brush it clean? It is never apart from right where one is. What is the use of going off here and there to practice?
>
> And yet, if there is the slightest discrepancy, the Way is as distant as

heaven from earth. If the least like or dislike arises, the Mind is lost in confusion. Suppose one gains pride of understanding and inflates one's own enlightenment, glimpsing the Wisdom that runs through all things, attaining the Way and, clarifying the Mind, raising an aspiration to escalate the very sky. One is making the initial, partial excursions about the frontiers but is still somewhat deficient in the vital Way of total emancipation.

Need I mention the Buddha, who was possessed of inborn knowledge? The influence of his six years of upright sitting is noticeable still. Or Bodhidharma's transmission of the mind-seal? The fame of his nine years of wall-sitting is celebrated to this day. Since this was the case with the saints of old, how can men of today dispense with negotiation of the Way?

You should therefore cease from practice based on intellectual understanding, pursuing words and following after speech, and learn the backward step that turns your light inwardly to illuminate yourself. Body and mind of themselves will drop away, and your original face will be manifest. If you want to attain suchness, you should practice suchness without delay.

It is a mistake to think that without zazen we will actualize Zen. However, zazen is not restricted to a particular sitting posture. If we really want to accomplish the Buddha Way, many years of training are necessary. With practice there is realization; with realization there is actualization. Without practice there is no true realization; without realization there is no actualization.

Only long and intensive training makes it possible to grasp the fact that Zen includes everything we do from morning until night. But whatever insight or awakening we may have had, if we stop doing zazen or don't sit enough, we are sure to get stuck in our realization. Our understanding will only stagnate as time goes by, crystallizing into something solid. Our life will then be based on a concept of reality rather than reality itself, and our idea of training will become merely trying to live up to our concept. We will watch ourself carefully to behave in accord with our picture of what we believe Zen practice should look like. This may appear to us as training, but it is just another idea.

The greater the realization the greater the chance of getting attached to it, so the only choice is continuous practice. Like the lobster we have to shed our shell over and over again in order to continue to grow. Whatever our realization is, eventually it hardens and becomes too limiting and cramped, it needs to be discarded. We become vulnerable once again before growing a new shell. The larger the lobster the more times it has had to shed its shell.

When we get stuck in great enlightenment we become even more dangerous to ourself and to others. We can stay stuck there for a long long time, even the rest of this life. If we are intelligent we drop our enlightenment before it drops us.

However some of us, like mayself, are not so wise and don't foresee our own fall. We ignore causation and attach to our experience of no-ego as the truth or reality. We are so convinced of our own greatness, and so confident in projecting it outward, that the possibility of losing it seems inconceivable.

Some of us who have gotten stuck here for decades may believe we have already come down off the mountain, because we have already had a fall. But there can be more than one descent: the first a partial one even by our own choosing, the second much greater. With the first we just land on a very large ledge. However, in order to progress we need to get all the way to the bottom. Those who haven't been through it may believe such a descent is a bad thing, that either we were never enlightened or that we are now worthless. This is far from the truth. In fact this is where we truly are just human beings living in our vulnerability, from here we can reach the people we are serving.

As some great masters have observed, throughout history there have been few teachers who really made it to the summit and then descended all the way to the bottom. Most get stuck somewhere along the way, because the thought that there truly is no escape and that we attain absolutely nothing on this journey is so fearful. It doesn't sell well in the West, probably not in the East either. We are all looking for a quick fix, a pill or a drink we can take to avoid the great effort necessary to attain the realization that there was never anything to be attained. Few want to face this simple truth.

There was never any self to attain it. If we believe or say that we have attained the incomparable and ungraspable Dharma Body, then what self would have attained it? If we say that we haven't attained it, then we are still believing that we are lacking something.

One old Master who did, and whom I appreciate more and more is Hyakujo, as we see him in the koan about the fox:

> An old man comes up to the front of the Dharma Hall after Hyakujo's talk and says, "A long time ago I was the abbot here and I was also called Hyakujo. A monk asked me does an enlightened person fall into causation or not, and I answered that an enlightened person does not. Because of this answer I was made to be reborn as a fox for five hundred lives. Now would you say a turning word that will release me from this fox's body?"
>
> Hyakujo replies, "Ask me the same question and I will answer it for you."
>
> The former Hyakujo repeats the question, and Hyakujo answers, "An enlightened person does not ignore causation."

The koan actually goes on, but what we can understand from here is that the former Hyakujo was just Hyakujo when he was many years younger, when he himself believed an enlightened person was free from karma. His misunderstanding is natural for one who is stuck in the absolute, because in the absolute there is no cause and effect, so one ends up denying the Law of Causation, karma.

Because of the karma he created by ignoring causation he suffered for many years. Hyakujo is warning us that a person who ignores cause and effect ends us up spending what can be seen as lifetimes as a fox, misleading students by saying that karma can be transcended, that one can be free from cause and effect. It makes sense that his understanding now is more mature than it was many years earlier when he was a young monk.

Two other Masters I appreciate more and more are Nangaku Ejo and his great successor Baso Doitsu. While walking through the monastery garden one day, he comes across Baso sitting there like a frog (Baso's nickname was Frog).

> Ejo asks, "What are you doing?"
> "What do you mean?" Baso answers, "I am sitting zazen of course."
> "What for?" Ejo asks.
> "To become a Buddha, of course," Baso says, "why else?"
> Ejo picks up two pieces of broken tile and begins to rub them together.

Baso looks over at him and says, "What are you doing?"

"What do you mean?" says Ejo, "I am trying to make a mirror, of course."

Baso says, "You can rub those two pieces of tile together forever and they will never become a mirror."

"You can sit there forever," Ejo replies, "and you will never become Buddha."

From this koan it is so clear that sitting or any other practice for that matter will not make us a Buddha. The question here is why? Baso was still seeking to become a Buddha not realizing that the very one sitting is Buddha.

Another koan makes the same point: "Daitzu Chisho Buddha sat on the Bodhi seat for ten thousand eons and did not attain Buddhahood. Why not?" Sitting even ten thousand eons did not make him into a Buddha; he was already an unrealized Buddha, sitting.

Zen is known as the Sudden School of Buddhism for just this reason. Whether one realizes it or not one is already a Buddha; either a realized Buddha or an unrealized Buddha. Realization is always sudden, actualization is always a gradual process. It only takes an instant to realize something, it is not a matter of time, though it may take a lifetime to truly actualize it.

Nansen and his disciple Joshu are two of my favorite Zen characters.

> Joshu, a young monk, only twenty years old at the time, asks his Master Nansen, "What is the Tao, the Way?"
>
> Nansen answers, "Ordinary mind is the Way."
>
> "If ordinary mind is the Way," Joshu asks, "then how do I attain it, how do I reach it?"
>
> "If you seek after the Tao, it only goes further and further away from you, you go further astray," Nansen answers.
>
> Joshu says, "Well then, how do I know that it is the Way?"
>
> Nansen replies, "The Way does not belong to either knowing or not-knowing. Knowing is illusion; not-knowing is a blankness. If you really attain to the Way of no-doubt, it is like the great void, so vast and boundless. How then can there be right and wrong in the Way?"
>
> At these words, Joshu is suddenly enlightened.

Here again a great master is telling us that our ordinary mind is it. There is nothing to attain. The Way is not extraordinary , it is just being ordinary and oneself. We don't want to hear this simple truth, we want to be extraordinary and special, we want to be great spiritual figures and guides, to teach others without going through the years of sincere discipline and training that Joshu and other great masters have endured.

When Joshu asks how he can seek the Way, Nansen tells him that to seek after it is only to go further away from it. As long as we are seeking it we are in our seeking mind, and not the Way. Of course we are always the Way, but we are restless and suffering because we feel separate from it.

Actually this too is the Way; it is only our dualistic notion that we are disconnected from our true nature, from God, from our own Divinity, that causes our suffering. This is the primordial itch that can't be scratched. Joshu then asks, if we do not try then how do we know that it is the Great Tao? Nansen clarifies by saying the Tao does not belong to knowing or not knowing, it transcends both knowing and not knowing.

I appreciate this point very much: the Tao doesn't belong to knowing, for knowing is delusion. In essential matters of life and death, our dualistic knowledge is the booby prize. It keeps us from digging deeper and truly resolving the great matter of life and death, from putting an end to seeking once and for all. We cease to be open and receptive, learning comes to a halt. We get stuck in knowing, in being an expert, and even try to teach others what we think we know.

Not knowing can take two forms: we can be like Emperor Wu after his encounter with Bodhidharma, confused and still seeking, or we can be stuck in the absolute, in a deep realization of not knowing, not responsible for our actions while ignoring cause and effect. Since we truly don't know, we don't seem to know right from wrong, good from bad, or simply how to act appropriately. However, when we come from the apex, beyond knowing and not knowing, we embrace both knowing and not knowing and go beyond being stuck in either. Our actions are appropriate to each situation. This is to truly be one with the Tao and in accord with the Way.

Much later in his life, when Joshu is quite old, sixty actually, his teacher Nansen dies. Joshu's been studying forty years, and still he feels he's not ready to teach, he hasn't ripened yet. How amazing is this, that after all these years of studying with the great Master Nansen, he still feels he needs to study further! And he makes a vow, an incredible vow if you really think about it. He says, I'm going to go out and try to deepen my practice, clarify the Way, and if I meet even an eight-year old child who has a better understanding and is clearer than I am, I will study with this child. However, if I meet even an eighty-year old who is not as clear as I am, I will share with them what I understand. He does this for another twenty years, until he's eighty years old, and at this point he realizes he's ready to teach.

Just look at that in comparison to those of us in our day and age, myself included, who feel we're ready to teach after a few years of Zen practice, many already teaching with less than ten or fifteen years of study. And how everyone wants to be a spiritual teacher, not realizing what an enormous responsibility it is to guide others, to take on the karmic responsibility of teaching.

Joshu had to be so sensitive and so aware. Perhaps he was dealing with feelings of being unqualified, or even unworthy. How beautiful this is, at sixty years of age until he's eighty, that he hesitates to represent or share the Dharma. Perhaps it is because he feels he is not yet clear enough, or that he is unworthy. But who is worthy? Are we worthy? What does it take to feel worthy of sharing the Dharma? Is it just our ego that feels worthy and ready? What does it really mean to carry the Dharma on, to hold the Dharma, to transmit the Dharma?

What incredible humility and confidence! It takes true confidence to be willing to open oneself up and surrender after studying Zen for more than forty years, to be so humble and patient, so unwilling to rush out and be a teacher or guru. These days here in the West, many with little or no true clarity or realization want to be teachers before being real students. How young and foolish I was at thirty-three, to feel that I was worthy!

Joshu is famous of course for the koans that come from later in his life. His *Mu*: "What is Buddha?" and Joshu says "Mu;" or "What is Buddha?" "The oak tree in the garden." His unique way of expressing his mastery of the teachings is beautifully illustrated in his references to the opening lines of the Third Chinese Patriarch's poem, the *Hsin hsin ming*: "The perfect Way is not difficult, just avoid picking and choosing."

> A monk once asked Joshu, "[You say] 'the supreme way is not dif- ficult, it simply dislikes choosing.' Isn't that a pit into which people today have fallen?"
> "Once someone asked me about that," Joshu replies, "since then, for five years, I haven't been able to apologize for it."

Have we as teachers been able to apologize enough for encour- aging students to give up picking and choosing, having preferences for or against things or others? Isn't this just another preference. How beautiful, this old Joshu's wisdom and humility.

> On another occasion Joshu spoke to his assembly, saying, "The real Way is not difficult. It only abhors choice and attachment. With but a single word there may arise choice and attachment or there may arise clarity. This old monk does not have that clarity. Do you appreciate the meaning of this or not?"
> Then a monk asked, "If you do not have that clarity, what do you appreciate?"
> "I do not know that either," Joshu answered.
> The monk asked again, "If you do not know, how can you say you do not have that clarity?"
> "Asking the question is good enough," Joshu replied, "now make your bows and leave."

There is so much to appreciate in this koan. Here Joshu says the real Way is not difficult, but only when we stop picking and choos- ing. We even need to stop having a preference for no preference. If we want to follow Joshu's example, we need to cease being attached not only to our likes and dislikes, but also to our preference for not being attached to our likes and dislikes.

Do we still hold preferences for and against people and things? Are we still attached to the company of those we love and wanting to get rid of those we despise? Do we still have a preference for life over death, wealth over poverty, awake over asleep, enlightened over deluded? If so, for us the perfect Way is difficult. Beyond that — and this is a point which I feel may not be appreciated by most Zen people — do we still crave and seek after liberation and want to get rid of our suffering? In other words, are we still clinging to our glimpses of reality, still attached to clarity? If so, we are not truly free like Master Joshu.

And when he's really old, somewhere in his hundreds — he lived till one hundred and twenty — there was an incident recorded in the koan called "Joshu's Stone Bridge." (Joshu's name came from the place in China where he settled, famous for its great stone bridge, which was known by the same name.)

> A young monk, full of vitality and arrogance, comes to visit old man Joshu and says, "I came here expecting to see the Great Stone Bridge of Joshu. But all I see is a broken down old wooden bridge. Where is this Great Stone Bridge of Joshu?"
> "It is because you can only see the old broken down wooden bridge," Joshu says, "that you can't see the Great Stone Bridge."
> "Where is this Great Stone Bridge?" the monk asks.
> "Right here in front of you," Joshu answers, "for asses and donkeys like yourself to cross over!"

His life was just that, for us all to pass over to the other shore. And we have to ask ourselves, what does that mean, to pass over? What is there to pass over? What is the other shore? Where are we going? We say, the Gateless Gate, *Mumonkan*. What gate? We have a koan about the buffalo passing through the window. Its head, horns, and four legs all pass through this lattice window, why is it that its tail gets stuck? What window, what is there to pass through? And yet when we pass through, why is the tail still stuck? What is this tail? What does it mean, that we never ever completely pass through? Is it because we are lacking some insight or is it a conscious vow? What is the meaning of the Zen circle that is never ever closed? That there's always more, always further to accomplish, more sentient beings to liberate, always further to ascend and to descend?

Look at these masters and what they had to go through to be ripened like Joshu or like Tokusan, to arrive at a place of so much humility and sweetness. Tokusan had been such a tough teacher. All long-time practitioners of Zen are well aware of Tokusan's killing sword, "Thirty Blows." "If you say a word of Zen, thirty blows! If you don't say a word of Zen, thirty blows!" Whatever you do, thirty blows. You're damned if you do and you're damned if you don't. How beautiful that is about our life. Whatever we do, we're going to receive life's blows. That's karma, and that ripens us.

Not that we are victims of our karma, which of course is nothing other than our life itself. There is no one, and no God, to blame. Cause and effect are truly one, not two. We cannot escape it; our karma is the teaching we need to relinquish to. Each time we do, our freedom increases and we discover deeper happiness, love and liberation.

Life smooths us out, like stones continuously tumbled and polished in a river. We can't know life until we've lived it, with all its ups and downs, its successes and failures. One thing about Zen that has always appealed to me is that it is not about staying on top of the mountain, but about descending from it, to live like a lotus in muddy water.

And yet, how painful are these falls, and how much the ascents inflate us and make us arrogant and full of pride. And what it takes to really ripen us! I've never ever experienced so much gratitude for these old masters and these old koans and for Zen itself, and just how amazing the process is, and yet how incredibly tough and difficult. It's Tokusan's Thirty Blows, it's our practice — and it is our beautiful life.

9

I Too Am Just A Stepping Stone

A few years ago I had a beautiful conversation with a young man I've known for quite a long time, which helped me realize something that deeply touches my heart. I feel like I'm at a point in my life, now that I'm past seventy and after what I have been through these past years, where my energy, and my drive, has shifted.

I used to say we should not stand in the shadow of our predecessors, or on their heads for that matter, but on their shoulders. Now what I am feeling is that I would like others to stand not in my shadow, or on my head, but on my shoulders. I'd like to assist them in deepening and clarifying their way, with the wisdom that I've learned from my rises and falls. There have been a couple now in my life, and each time of course it's devastating and it's heartbreaking, but it's also an experience of learning, maturing and softening.

In the past, particularly from 1999 until 2011, my life was really about trying to change the world, awakening and raising the consciousness of the planet. That's still there, but I no longer wish to do it in the grand way I was doing it before. What I would like to do now is serve those who really want to serve others in making a difference. Of course I want to make a difference — however I want to be more of a support to those who have the energy and the capacity to change the world for the better, whether they are Zen practitioners or not.

Maezumi Roshi used to say he was just a stepping stone. I too am just a stepping stone, for those who want to bring the teaching forward. The enthusiasm I heard in that phone conversation, the beautiful vision and eagerness to help others as well as the frustrations that I often hear in similar conversations, inspire me to want to help them in doing their work and manifesting their vision for the sake of this world.

These days I feel more like a grandparent, savoring and wanting to encourage the vitality and vision of the younger generation. I realize that I am not as available as I once was, less like a parent but more like a grandfather who can be there for the grandchildren, to offer guidance and hopefully some experienced wisdom and support when needed.

I realized some time in the past few years that my way, what I have always seemed most able to do, is to help people awaken and clarify the Way, rather than directing them how to actualize it in their particular life and work. What I'm best at is helping them become more aware and conscious and go deeper in their practice; then the actualization becomes more their work, their koan — how do they bring this realization into manifestation in their daily life?

I think this is true of many Zen Masters. There are people who are really good at setting up systems and structures and I'd love to be able to do that, but that's not my forte. Helping others become clearer, to see places where they may be stuck, or to remove obstacles that may be hindering them from fully actualizing their realization — that I can do, and really want to do.

WHAT IS ZEN PRACTICE?

10

The Middle Way

Not all of what we might call the bones that need to be spit out were part of the original fish. Some were added to the dish as it was being served here in the West. In other words, they were not the Buddhist teachings themselves, but the translation and interpretation of them which took root in our culture. One of these is the very common term we have for Buddhism itself, the Middle Way.

The Buddha taught the Middle Way as the fourth of the Four Noble Truths, also known as the Eightfold Path to relieve suffering and attain liberation. It is often thought of as simply a narrow Path between two extremes, but I think this is a significant misunderstanding of the Buddha's meaning, and actually a far cry from the wisdom and compassion of his teaching.

Here again the image of a triangle is a useful device. At the bottom left corner we have the Hinayana, meaning the lesser or narrow vehicle, which I prefer to call a literal interpretation of right and wrong, good and bad, self and other, not to be confused with the Theravada School of Buddhism. At the bottom right hand corner of the triangle we have what in Zen is referred to as the Buddhayana or One Mind / One Body vehicle. This is the absolute or non-dual perspective, beyond right and wrong, good and bad, self and other. To understand this perspective requires a breakthrough from dualistic thinking, going beyond the conceptual thinking mind. This is usually referred to as a *kensho* or *satori* or enlightenment.

The apex of the triangle, as I see it, is the Middle Way, also known as the Mahayana or great vehicle. This signifies that the Middle Way both embraces the Hinayana and the Buddhayana perspectives and transcends them. In the Zen tradition these are known as the Three Yanas or Vehicles. Since the Apex is not attached to either the Hinayana or Buddhayana perspective it is free to be appropriate in any situation, to respond with wisdom and manifest as compassion. When it is true wisdom, Prajna wisdom, beyond non-discriminating and discriminating wisdom, it always functions as compassion. Here there is no blame towards oneself or anyone or anything else. Here you are being your true self embodying what you already are to begin with.

When we realize that these three points of the triangle are not static but in a continuous flow, always revolving, we have what I call Vajrayana, the free movement of energy with no yana or vehicle higher or lower, greater or less than any other. It is not, as is often thought, that Vajrayana (the Diamond Vehicle) is the highest teaching, with Mahayana lesser and Hinayana the least. It is that Vajrayana is the non-static whole dynamic, a brilliantly, energetic, indestructible teaching, like Mahayana only constantly revolving and manifesting the three yanas. It is always thus; we just don't realize it is.

With this understanding, consider the first of the Eightfold Path. It is often called 'right view,' but could be better translated as 'complete or whole view or understanding.' Complete view is that there is no static view that is the right view, that all views are partial and incomplete. The same is true for the second, so-called right thought or intention. Complete thought is beyond thinking and not thinking; it is non-thinking, always moving and flowing between thinking and not thinking. Again, it is our most natural state of being. We can see each of the other six of the Eightfold Path in a similar way.

This means we are not trying to keep to some narrow path or balance precariously on a razor's edge between right and wrong. Such an understanding only leads to contraction, frustration, internal conflict, repression and dysfunction. When we see the Path this narrowly, with the Middle Way as a fine line that we living in constant fear of falling off, it is like binding ourselves without so much as a rope.

When we disown large and essential parts of our selves, our actions arise not from true wisdom and compassion but from fear and a dualistic notion of a separate and fixed self. Rather than living freely in the present moment we are bound by predetermined judgements about right and wrong, good and bad, and concepts of self and other implanted by our culture, parents, teachers and society in general. Rather than seeing that all things are empty and unsubstantial, that all form is formless, we are living as though what is happening is permanent, real, solid, and substantial. It is as though we are in a dream and instead of awakening from it we are trying to get others to enter our dream and rescue us. We become the victims of our own delusion, and feeling the powerlessness of a victim, we strike out at others, actively or passively, sometimes even believing we are helping or rescuing them.

From the perspective of the Apex or Mahayana Path there is no absolute right or wrong, only a relative and appropriate way to be according to our position, time, and place. What is appropriate is determined by these conditions and also by the degree or amount of our action, neither too much nor too little. All things are impermanent and constantly changing. Our fear and denial of this basic truth is what causes our suffering and lack of real freedom. True freedom only comes when we drop the illusory beliefs and concepts that bind us.

When we come from the Apex or Middle Way we do not deny either the relative or absolute reality but embrace the two as one. We are conscious and aware of our emotions, thoughts and sensations as well as their empty nature. When each perspective or voice within us is fully owned and embodied and all are worked with dynamically as the perfect manifestation of Buddha as Dharma, this, in my view, is Vajrayana. This is where our karma is manifested as our Dharma (teaching), our Dharma is no other than our karma. All emotions, thoughts and sensations are seen as perfect manifestations of Reality (Buddha).

Here, however, there is a further pitfall, which illustrates once again how we can be misled — and delude ourselves — by our interpretation of the teachings. I know this one well because I fell deeply into it myself. This was one of the things I mentioned earlier that I had to learn the hard way. It has to do with what we mean when we speak about fully owning and embodying each voice within us.

In January of 2005 I was struggling and probably somewhat off balance because of the recent sudden death of our beloved dog Tiby and my own close encounter with death from cancer just a year and a half earlier. Most likely because of these personal challenges I consciously took on a practice based on my understanding of the teaching that I needed to embrace and go beyond all opposites, to embody all extremes — good and bad, right and wrong, saint and sinner, enlightened and deluded — and transcend them.

It was out of this experience that my concept of the Apex emerged a year later, since I felt that in embodying the extremes I was literally being pushed to a higher place that included and yet transcended them, which I have since been calling the Apex.

Sadly, what I didn't realize until April 2011 is that there is a crucial difference between owning the extremes and acting them out. Being out of tune with my own better judgement, I simply didn't make the necessary distinction between embodying and manifesting.

This mistake coupled with my still being to some extent stuck in the absolute and clinging to feelings of entitlement made for a toxic mix. It gave me a license to behave in ways that most people would immediately see as harmful. But I was in some sort of denial of the damage I was causing others and myself by my not having clear boundaries and my detachment from others' vulnerability as well as my own. As I have said before, deeply rooted patterns are a bitch, and it is easy to get stuck in them especially when they are self-serving.

At the end of April 2011, working with my mentors Hal and Sidra Stone, I finally realized I had misunderstood the teaching of embodying the extremes. I also began to see more clearly the ways in which my four decades of concentrating on the spiritual had impaired my own personal development. I saw that my life was out of balance because of this misunderstanding which led me to act out in ways that I should not have. I had gotten stuck in a particular way of viewing the teaching for myself. To own, embody and empower an aspect of the self does not mean to act that behavior out when it is going to create harm to others.

This understanding of the Middle Way is inclusive and expansive rather than limiting and narrow. Even though in the absolute reality there appears to be no choice since all is karma, it does not deny that we have preferences and choice and can exercise discernment. We take full responsibility for our actions and reactions, for cause and effect, and are accountable for our choices in this life whether conscious or unconscious.

11

The Arhat and the Bodhisattva

For some time now I have been questioning whether we Mahayana Buddhists — Zen, Tibetan and others — ought to re-look at our concept of the Arhat, the one who seeks self-realization and complete emancipation for him- or herself. I wrote about the subject several years ago, but since then the significance of the Arhat and its relevance to my own life and my view of the direction of Buddhism and Zen practice in the West has come into sharper focus for me.

From the Mahayana perspective, the Arhat and the Bodhisattva are the two principal archetypes of Buddhist practice and aspiration, representing the key difference between the Theravada and Mahayana schools of Buddhism. In order to accentuate the difference and, not incidentally to elevate the Mahayana, we view the Theravada school as idealizing the Arhat whose practice towards the attainment of nirvana is to free him- or herself from greed, hatred and ignorance. We Mahayana Buddhists, on the other hand, see ourselves as aspiring to a higher spiritual ideal: the Bodhisattva who vows to postpone his or her own complete liberation for the sake of all sentient beings.

I now understand that this is an oversimplification and misrepresentation of actual Theravada teachings, that in fact the Bodhisattva has been there in Theravada from the time of the Buddha, and that the notion of a self-centered Arhat is in many ways a straw man.

However, the way we distinguish and judge these two archetypes of spiritual practice, the Arhat and the Bodhisattva, is itself very revealing. We tend to see them as antithetical or even mutually exclusive and opposed to each other. But I have become increasingly convinced that we need to acknowledge that we all embody both, and that we need not see them as conflicting within ourselves. In my opinion they actually complement and support each other, and each enables the other to fully realize its nature and its function in our life.

We Mahayanists often see the Arhat's path, seeking personal liberation from samsara, as selfish and inferior to our Bodhisattva path of putting others before ourselves. Some of us even regard the Arhat's aspiration to personal liberation as not very enlightened. I myself held this view very early on. The moment the Bodhisattva vow arose within me in '71, I disowned a number of personal traits and attitudes, voices within me that I deemed more egotistical and self-serving, since the vow to liberate all sentient beings before my own complete liberation was so strong and seemed so much more selfless and heroic than the Arhat's.

Judging the Arhat, this aspect of self within me, as more egoistic and self-centered, I preferred to see myself as a Bodhisattva. I can now see that this put my life out of balance. This is a common phenomenon in Western spiritual practices, seeing the ego's needs as bad and even evil and working to get rid of it, as if we ever could. Push down the ego and it only comes out in covert ways, as mine did.

Not that I was consciously banishing the Arhat within me; I saw it more as identifying with the Bodhisattva, embracing his noble qualities. It was not until I began to realize how deeply I had buried the Arhat within myself, and started to bring him back into my life, that I recognized how the Arhat disowned had been coming out in my life in covert ways. Inevitably these ways were what I would now call unhealthy, immature and irresponsible, but I couldn't see them while the Arhat was disowned.

While I was consciously putting others first, identifying myself as a Bodhisattva, I didn't see how I unconsciously became quite self-important and full of myself, and how I rationalized my sexual misconduct. At the same time, because my vow to liberate all sentient beings before my own liberation played such a powerful role in my life, I often did not take good care of my family or myself.

I now see that disowning the Arhat within me had a subtle but pervasive and profound effect on my life throughout my years of traditional Zen practice, all the way back to '72. I feel that I had a tacit understanding, based on what I was taught and what I believed through my realizations, that my practice was not about being happy. My life and vow was to bring all sentient beings to the other shore before myself. My own happiness would have to wait.

Since I saw my loved ones, wife and kids as extensions of myself, their happiness was not always a priority for me either. This was also true of my teacher Maezumi Roshi. When he came to America in his mid-twenties he made a vow to always put others before himself, and once he had a wife and children this also applied to them. I remember him often saying to me, "Our practice is not to be happy." He himself always felt he put others first, which I believe is what in the end resulted in his premature death. He never took time for himself or for his family. Just two months before his death many doctors and healers said he was totally exhausted.

By January 2011 I was exhausted and felt overburdened with all the responsibilities I was carrying. It was as if I had been a lifeguard all my life swimming out to rescue others and now after my fall I found myself drowning and in such big surf that all I could manage was to rescue myself. I was forced to let the others go, it was up to them to find their way back to shore. I was powerless to do any more, I had to just give up trying to save everyone else.

With a lot of soul-searching I began to resurrect the Arhat from the life of oblivion down in the basement to which I, like so many of my fellow Zen students and my teacher, had consigned him. Acknowledging my actual exhaustion and unhappiness I was able to admit and appreciate that part of me which does seek happiness, peace and freedom, without judging myself to be selfish or egocentric for not always putting others first.

I realized that the Arhat couldn't help me when his hands and feet were tied and mouth gagged down in the basement. As long as I saw this aspect of myself as unworthy I was blind to how it could serve me, and how my attitude towards him was effecting my life in negative ways.

The Arhat owned, embodied and empowered now allows me to pay more attention to my own meditation practice, not only to seek further clarification but also to take responsibility for my own happiness and liberation. It also has allowed me to make time for my close relations, family, loved ones, and myself. I have been able to find peace for myself and let others be responsible for their own lives. I can own my karma, no longer coming from the mindset of the victim but taking full responsibility for my own life.

For the first time since beginning traditional Zen training in '72, I have been taking better care of myself. I am sitting, enjoyably, many hours every day, much more than when the Arhat was disowned. I appreciate all that life offers me, and try not to take anything for granted. My life is filled with more joy than I ever experienced in all my years of traditional Zen. Of course traditional Zen is what got me to this place and I appreciate it as the foundation of my practice. However, after arriving here I had to stop carrying that raft around on my back and leave it behind.

By owning the Arhat I was able to see the narrowness of the view which elevates the Mahayana as the 'great vehicle' and belittles the Arhat as representing the Hinayana, or 'lesser vehicle.' Like other seemingly opposite voices they are actually complementary and inseparable from one another. When I acknowledge both, my wish is to awaken all sentient beings before my own complete enlightenment, and my vow to continue to refine my life is even stronger than before.

From this perspective, which I call the Apex, embracing both, I appreciate at a much subtler and deeper level than I did before that all are Buddhas and I can simply allow them to be themselves. They are all perfect just as they are. I can honor their own intrinsic power and capacity. It is not necessary to control, judge or always teach them as if they lack something. I can let go of needing to control or judge what my successors and students are doing, and just let them be. This has given them the opportunity to stand on their own two feet and to be more independent. I am able sit and be still, to be rather than do, to enjoy this precious life rather than run around trying to save the world.

Coming most of the time from the Apex, I am the one truly in charge of this life, no longer run by either the Bodhisattva or the Arhat within me. They are always present and accessible but no longer working out of balance without my consent. I am now free to seek further clarification and to work on my own shadows as well as to work for the liberation of all sentient beings, without feeling that the Arhat within me is somehow inferior to the Bodhisattva. They are both absolutely necessary aspects of this human life.

12

Five Maps of the Path

In the Zen tradition, some of the most creative and skillful teachings have been offered in the form of maps of the Path left for us by wise and compassionate teachers who have gone on ahead of us. I would like to share with you five of the more traditional Paths, in the language that I was taught them, with the understanding that 'the map is not the territory.' Of course, since they cover the same territory and I am describing them from my perspective, they overlap and duplicate each other in some respects, but each offers distinctive and significant insights that can be useful in clarifying the Way for those on the Path to supreme and ultimate awakening, *Anuttara Samyak Sambodhi*.

I. THE PARABLE OF ENYADATTA

The ancient tale of Enyadatta is a good metaphor for our journey in Zen practice. This story was told by the Buddha himself and is briefly mentioned in the Surangama Sutra. I like to embellish it a little when I tell it:

Enyadatta was a beautiful lady, the mother of two children. One day she was invited to a birthday party at some good friends' home and, since she didn't get out much, she decided to find a babysitter for her children and go to the party. She got very drunk that evening and returned home late.

Her kids were angry that she left them with a babysitter so they decided to play a trick on her. They turned the glass of her mirror around so that when she awoke the next morning, very hung over, and looked into it, there was no reflection to be seen. In her hung-over state she thought her head was missing. She began searching for it all over the bedroom, under the bed, behind the chair, and when she couldn't find it in the house she ran outside and searched for it there.

Poor Enyadatta, frantic to find her head, ran through the neighborhood, screaming and crying. "I've lost my head! I've lost my head, please help me!" She ran all the way back to the house where the party had been held and began demanding that her friend help her find her head. "Enyadatta," her friend said, "you are crazy. You haven't lost your head, it's right where it's always been!" "No, no, no! I've seen for myself that it's missing, and I've got to find it. What ever will I do without my head?"

Her friend saw that Enyadatta was in a strange state of mind, so she tied her to a chair and tried to convince her she was not really missing her head, that she was really OK. Still she struggled and fought, desperate to break free. "Let me go," she cried, "I've got to find my head!"

Her friend tried everything she could think of to calm her down, insisting Enyadatta was missing nothing, that she was absolutely perfect, complete and whole just as she was, but it was all in vain. Finally, her friend slapped Enyadatta, and at that moment she realized that she had her head and it was right where it belonged.

She started shouting all over again — only now she was completely ecstatic. "My head, my head, I found my head!" Still fearing for Enyadatta's sanity, her friend kept her tied to the chair, hoping she would calm down. "Just sit there!" she told her, and then left for a while. Enyadatta sat for what seemed like a very long time, and gradually returned to her calm self. Then her friend let her go.

Enyadatta went home and resumed her daily routine, but was still in a strange state, still excited about finding what had never been lost in the first place. Now she felt kind of superior to other people because she had found her head and others hadn't yet discovered theirs. She even tried to convince family and friends to look for their heads.

Over time she began to realize that this was insane. So the

excitement faded and eventually she was able to return to her ordinary life, almost as if nothing had happened. But of course, something had happened — she had gone through an incredible experience.

In our life, before the awakening of the Bodhi mind, the mind that seeks the Way, we are like Enyadatta before she looked in the mirror on that fateful morning — we see things dualistically. We feel either good or bad, adequate or inadequate, superior or inferior to others. We worry a lot about what others think or say about us, we feel bad when criticized and happy when praised. We compare and judge other people as either better or worse than ourselves; we put others down or become envious and jealous when we feel they are better off than we are. We can't seem to stop comparing and judging everything and everyone we encounter.

This habit comes from the dualistic way we look at the world. We're slaves of our dualistic minds, caught up in our thoughts, feelings, and emotions. On and on, we pass from one realm to another, from happiness to depression, from contentment to frustration, anger, and resentment, from special to unworthy. This suffering is created by our own minds. When we feel that we can bear it no longer, we begin to search for a way out.

Like Enyadatta, at some point in our lives we also may realize that something is off, something seems to be missing. We try different ways to lessen our pain, hoping to somehow make our lives better. Sometimes things actually seem better for a while, but it doesn't last.

Sooner or later we fall back into our discontent and frustration. Inwardly we still feel incomplete, unworthy and inadequate, so we keep searching for a way to feel whole. We begin by looking nearby, in familiar places. Eventually our search may lead us far from home, even to other countries and cultures. We can end up traveling thousands of miles trying to find 'It.'

Our destiny changes when we finally encounter the practice of sitting meditation. We learn to sit down and shut up long enough to turn our light inward. At first, though, it's a struggle. Our mind is undisciplined, it comes up with all sorts of ideas and chases after all kinds of things. We realize that instead of riding the waves of life, we are being tumbled and crushed by our thoughts and emotions. We obviously have no control of our experience, and we don't have a clue how to master it. In despair, we may wonder if we will ever find peace of mind.

With perseverance and good karma, we may meet someone, perhaps a teacher who says, "You don't lack anything. You are complete, whole and perfect as you are. In fact, you are awakened, a Buddha!" But at first we can't hear this because our own experience tells us we are incomplete and certainly not perfect. Every time I look at myself, I see how inadequate and unworthy I am.

Other people appear to be much better off than me — more together, more confident, more enlightened. Any trust or confidence I manage to build is easily shaken. When life puts me to the test, my self-confidence is exposed as the act it really is, and I'm reminded again just how incomplete and insufficient I am. I may feel unworthy and vulnerable and put up walls and defenses so others, and life, can't get to me. To believe that nothing is lacking seems like fantasy, or worse, insane.

The turning point comes when someone — or life — slaps us in the face. In that moment, we cut through the apparent reality and realize that nothing ever was missing. Our deluded view only made it seem so. Suddenly we can see our wholeness and perfection — the absolute side of reality. We realize, in Master Dogen's words, "Enlightenment is intimacy with all things."

Just a glimpse of the absolute makes us ecstatic. We get high on the experience and forget all about the relative side of reality. So the next thing to arise is arrogance. We believe we have or can see something others can't. Our view seems so profound, we doubt that anyone has ever experience anything like it.

When this happened to the great Master Hakuin, he proclaimed that no one since the time of Shakyamuni Buddha, had had as clear an experience as his. Even the Buddha proclaimed, "I alone am the World Honored One."

Yet the Buddha's realization was unique. He could see immediately that not only was he perfect and whole, so was everyone else.

For some, it takes a lot of time and practice to go from the realization "I am It," to the insight "so is everyone else."

Even after realization, sitting is essential because we can easily get stuck in the absolute perspective. Previously we were stuck in delusion before enlightenment; now we are deluded, and stuck, in enlightenment. We are living in a state of grace where everything is perfect as it is. Every snowflake falls in the right spot because we have no preconceived ideas or preferences of where it should fall. Everything has meaning because we're not looking for any meaning. In this state we can do no wrong; everything is perfect.

Now, if you think about this while you are in a relative state of mind, red flags pop up right away. It's dangerous to believe that everything you do is perfect, beyond all judgements of right and wrong. Yet from the absolute state of mind, this is the simple truth.

So in this phase of our practice, we may fall into a big trap — the delusion of enlightenment. Everything we do is in harmony with the Buddha-Dharma. We may disregard dualistic views of right and wrong, good and bad, nothing seems to matter and we may think we can do whatever we want.

We ignore the law of cause and effect — karma — which operates on the relative level, where what we do really does matter. Everything counts, not only our actions and words but also our thoughts and attitude. In the absolute, there is no cause and effect, so we go on blindly, creating more and more karma. Yet the absolute and the relative are two sides of the same coin and they can't be separated. If you screw up in the relative world, the absolute won't save you.

Inevitably we become attached to the absolute state of mind, and this attachment stops us from moving ahead willingly. Now we are stuck in the enlightened view that I am perfect, complete and whole as I am. Why let go of bliss when the memory of hell is so fresh? We recognize that other people are still living in duality — judging, evaluating, condemning and comparing, literally creating hell for themselves — and we remember it well.

Now that we've made it to the top of the mountain, we don't want to go back down. Just the thought of returning to the world of samsara and all the suffering that goes with it brings up resistance and clinging. Yet life goes on and eventually we see that there is really no choice. Karma catches up with us and we can no longer continue to be blind and ignore the harm we've been causing. It's time to pay for all the karma we have created and we either voluntarily or, more likely, not so voluntarily descend or fall off the mountain.

It takes tremendous faith and courage to let go of the enlightened view and go back into a state of complete delusion. The enlightened view feels so much higher, beyond all dualistic thinking, beyond our normal state of delusion. We are liberated, because even though we may still experience pain and suffering, we know there is no self and no one to suffer. Yet finally, we return to our ordinary view. We go beyond delusion within enlightenment and arrive at delusion beyond delusion. Conventional perception returns and we see things the same way everybody else does.

We're back to square one, the world of suffering. But there is a subtle difference: since we have been one with the awakened mind, it has not been truly lost. After going through this process many times, we learn how to move freely between the dualistic and the non-dualistic views. Life eventually becomes much more joyous and fulfilling, we appreciate the simple things in life and are happy just being who we are.

There is no need to look for a head that was never missing nor to encourage others to look for theirs. However if someone believes they are missing their head we do what we can to help them discover the truth that they are just fine as they are. From this place of knowing that nothing is missing and we are OK as we are we simply refine who we are, becoming a little kinder towards those around us, more loving and compassionate towards all.

Zen practice goes in spirals, one phase simply follows another. When we look ahead, there is always further to go. And if we've reached the summit, there is always another mountain to climb. We have to descend and climb up the next one, over and over again.

Dogen Zenji taught that the first step is to raise the Bodhi mind, the mind that wishes to clarify this life. Like Enyadatta, we need to see that something is missing. Our feelings of incompleteness, pain and suffering become the motivation to practice. Then, a slap in the face brings us awakening, liberation, and peace. But we can't stay there, and eventually we have to raise the Bodhi-mind once again, practice, realize, nirvana, drop it — over and over again.

Because the deluded mind can only think in limited terms, it wants to find a conclusion or a finish line. The dualistic mind is simply too small to fathom infinity or eternity; when we can fathom infinity, we're not using the deluded mind — in fact, we're completely out of our mind. When the small contracted mind lets go, we experience Buddha, the awakened Mind.

Some spiritual paths seem to end at the top of the mountain, and perhaps some people manage to stay there believing that is superior to descending the mountain. But the Zen path is the practice of the Bodhisattva — what I call the path of the human being. After realization, we knowingly choose to return to being human. We didn't really have a choice before; we were stuck in duality, in the realm of suffering.

Now, having traveled the entire circle, we can make a conscious choice to be an ordinary human being who has awakened and yet chooses to return to the world to help others: a Bodhisattva. How many people can we reach from the top of a mountain? To help other human beings, we have to come down to the earth, to be like a lotus in muddy water. This is where the Bodhisattva can make a difference.

II. The Five Reasons We Practice Meditation. Plus One.

1. Mindfulness Meditation

We practice mindfulness meditation to become healthier and happier, physically, emotionally, psychologically, spiritually and mentally. It improves our mood, decreases stress, and boosts our immune system. Mindfulness involves being aware moment to moment of our subjective conscious experience.

We see that we are not our thoughts, feelings or sensations and free ourself from these notions and attachments to self. We learn to focus our unwieldy and scattered mind on the present, settling it down by paying attention to breath, thoughts, sensations and actions without judging ourself.

We become more aware of our mind's tendency to be like a wild horse or a monkey jumping from tree to tree, and learn to tame it and bring it to some peace by focusing and concentrating on one thing at a time. Most of us begin here, seeking to improve our life in one way or another; for some it can lead to further depths of practice.

2. The Power of Samadhi

The second reason we practice meditation is to cultivate the power of samadhi, which develops in the lower belly about two to three inches below the navel. We also call this *joriki* which means the power and energy of samadhi. At this stage it is less about being mindful than about becoming one with the object of our concentration.

Our practice shifts to a one-pointed concentration to penetrate deeply into the self. We may still believe that the self and others do exist, but we develop a certain intuition and understanding of the nature of reality and gain more distance from and less attachment to the self. We become one with deeper states of samadhi and realize some powers that we had been totally unaware of. We can stay focused on a task without getting scattered or lost, and develop a centeredness and equanimity beyond what we had cultivated with our mindfulness practice.

We may yet not have a strong sense of seeking awakening. Our meditation is more about obtaining something that makes us feel more powerful and better about ourself, and still lacks the Bodhi Mind, the mind that seeks or aspires to the Way.

3. Seeking Liberation for Oneself

The third reason for meditation arises from the mind that seeks the Way. For the first time our Path becomes a Buddhist one, a Path of awakening. The two previous stages, however spiritual they seemed, were not truly Buddhist. Here one enters the Path of enlightenment where the goal is nothing less than to liberate oneself from the bonds that keep us in this self-made prison and to be free from suffering.

This practice is usually referred to as the small vehicle or Hinayana, as opposed to the great vehicle or Mahayana, because it accommodates only oneself, like a bicycle rather than a bus. We continue to use various forms of meditation such as mindfulness, koans, following the breath, and sitting to attain our goal of self-liberation.

Still, no matter how much we meditate we are simply unable to trust in a reality where all existence is an inseparable whole, each one of us embracing the cosmos in its totality. We still divide the world into good and evil, right and wrong, and therefore long to escape from our suffering and dissatisfaction.

4. The Great Way

The fourth reason we meditate is to awaken and practice for the sake of all sentient beings. This is the truly altruistic Mahayana Path, the great rather than the narrow or literal vehicle. We sit for the sake of others, putting aside seeking our own complete liberation, offering up our meditation and samadhi to awaken them all.

We knowi that we will never truly be liberated from suffering as a species or a world until every last sentient being is liberated. Like the buffalo passing through the window, our tail is so long it extends to all sentient beings. Dualistic thoughts and judgements have been seen through, body and mind dropped off.

5. The Supreme Way

Here we just sit in great faith with no goal or aim in our meditation, in a state of mind where we do not seek to obtain something nor get attached to any object. Universal wisdom is rooted in this state of mind. It transcends dualities and limitations created by our egoistic mind. Here we lose all, we are free and happy.

This acting without wanting to achieve a result, and giving freely without wanting something in return is one of the most difficult states for us in the West to understand. We tend to think in terms of profit, "If I give someone something, maybe they will give me something in return". True meditation is not practiced with a hope to personally profit, for a reward or to obtain esoteric powers.

We are aware and certain that our sitting itself is the actualization of our true nature, and therefore there is no striving. We sit for the sake of sitting, with no ambition, knowing that we are already perfect, complete and whole and that there is absolutely nothing lacking or extra, nothing to attain and no place to go. We sit with whatever arises, fulfilled and happy, relaxed and natural, without preference or judgements.

Liberated from the need to be clear and awakened, we are no longer trying to get rid of our confusion or delusion. We are at peace with ourself and the world. Whatever we are engaged in we do completely, leaving no trace behind.

Our samadhi is empowering all beings and those receptive to it drink of its nectar, so we alternate between the fourth and fifth levels, responding appropriately to each situation as it arises.

6. All Ways / No Way: Continuous and Endless Practice

Sixth and yet not sixth. Here we sit for all of the five previous reasons with no preference among them. We sit to improve our self on all levels, to refine our life and every aspect of it, for deeper states of samadhi as well as to further liberate ourself and others — and for no damned reason at all.

We simply sit because we love to sit and it is just who we are. It is as if we are pulled by a force greater than ourself deeper and deeper into a silk-like samadhi of joy and bliss. Our everyday life and meditation are neither the same nor different, there is no difference between deluded or enlightened and yet there is.

Here we realize that just as we could not leave any sentient being behind for the sake of our own liberation, we cannot leave any aspect of the self unawakened either. Our continuous, endless practice is to awaken all aspects of our self, bringing them from unawakened to awakened, immature to mature, unhealthy to healthy.

Here one is like a lotus flower in muddy water, like the hazy moon on a beautiful cloudy night, sometimes appearing bright and clear, sometimes even dull or dim. At times one can be mistaken for an ordinary person, at other times for an exceptional being, sometimes deluded and sometimes enlightened, sometimes confused and other times clear and amazing.

Here there is no longer the stink of Zen. In a room full of people no one would see that we are Zen through and through. Any appearance of being 'spiritual' is gone and what remains is an ordinary person with great depth and clarity, truly happy and at peace.

III. Zen Master Ummon's Two Sicknesses

In many spiritual traditions the Path is seen as a progression of stages, a journey advancing from less to more awareness and ever-deepening realization. The great Master Ummon offers another view of the Path as a recurring cycle of pitfalls or 'sicknesses,' two sicknesses that prevent the light from penetrating clearly before great realization and two afterwards. Each of these, Ummon's warning us, is a place where we need to be careful not to get stuck.

"The first sickness is where everything is unclear, and something seems to hang before you. Therefore, the light does not penetrate."

We have experienced enlightenment, but not yet a great realization, so we are still stuck in our dualistic view of the world and ourself, and therefore unclear. Something seems to be an obstacle before us that we must penetrate, but we are unable to do so.

We have not yet opened our eyes to a world in which the totality is oneself. It is very difficult to give up our tightly held view that the world and oneself are separate. Therefore, the light does not penetrate completely.

Whenever the light is cut off we return to darkness and our deluded way of perceiving reality. We can't help thinking that there is an objective world in dualistic opposition to us. We separate everything into subject and object, self and other, me and you. We divide things into good and bad, right and wrong, superior and inferior. The objective world has not yet been clearly penetrated as having no ultimate substance.

We have had a taste of the absolute while we are still abiding in the relative. This first glimpse changes our perspective on life, therefore our life itself. However we fall back into duality over and over again. Our first glimpse can range from a slight awakening to such a profound opening that it may be mistaken for a great enlightenment unless checked and verified by a true master.

"The second sickness is where you have realized that everything is void, but still you feel you are in a mist. Therefore the light does not penetrate thoroughly."

We have realized that everything is empty and unsubstantial but still feel we are in a fog and not clear. Therefore the light still does not penetrate thoroughly. We practice surrendering to the Way and yet the light still does not completely penetrate. We are at a loss and confused, still doubting our realization and attainment.

We may even go into great doubt, doubting everything, ourself, our teacher and the teachings, even that there is any enlightenment or escape from our suffering, and therefore we despair. We have not yet dropped the bottom out and so we are still more like cup than a conduit. The Dharma does not flow freely through us.

"In the Dharma Body there are also two sicknesses. First, if you reach the Dharma, but fall and remain there, and do not extinguish your own opinion about it, that is one sickness."

At this stage we have clearly realized that the subjective and objective world are empty, but with this great realization we get stuck in the absolute, denying the relative, or apparent reality. We are one with all things, but we are not seeing others as separate and independent.

Here we can fall into denial of cause and effect, karma. We remain attached to that world of enlightenment, to the Dharma, to the truth. There is still a self attached to its views and its experience. This is the sickness known as Dharma attachment.

"Second, if you think it is wrong to give up efforts after enlightenment, and minutely examine your own consciousness, and find there is no scar, that is a sickness."

This is the second sickness following true realization. Here we have fallen from our attachment to absolute reality, and find that we have finally arrived back in relative reality and are no longer stuck. Believing that we have let go of our attachment to enlightenment and pride, and returned to being an ordinary person, we feel there is no further refinement to be done. This too becomes a place where we get stuck and it is another sickness.

IV. THE FOUR OBSTACLES, OR THE WISDOM OF NO ESCAPE

Another map highlights four key obstacles or enemies to actualizing the Path. These may be recognizable to those familiar with shamanism, though they are by no means unique to the shamanistic tradition. I've borrowed and explained them in my own way from my own experience of each. We will all eventually encounter each of them as we continue on the Way. However, the method of confronting these obstacles in some shamanistic practices is to defy them; in my view, the Zen approach is quite different, it is to embrace and transcend.

1. Fear

The first obstacle or enemy we face on the Path is fear, which of course is there before we begin practice as well as after we raise the mind that aspires to seek the Way. When we first begin to look inward, to study the self, and seek wisdom, power, peace, and freedom, many fears arise. As we face and acknowledge them we have the opportunity to transform or flip them from negative to positive, from unhealthy to healthy. When we face, own and embody them, our fears transcend themselves and become attentiveness and awareness, a keen ability to observe and clearly see what is.

When we go through the barrier of our fear, own, embody, and empower it to serve its purpose, it flips into realization, clarity and wisdom. Our final fear before this major breakthrough comes in the form of great doubt, the fear of being completely alone, without anyone or anything to rely or depend on, no one who can finally tell us we are OK as we are.

With this breakthrough we reach a state of profound clarity and wisdom. We see the interconnectedness and interdependence, the oneness and perfection of all things. We see that I and all things are perfect, whole and complete — no exception, nothing lacking, nothing extra.

All is perfect, complete and whole just as it is. What I do affects you and the entire world, and what you do affects me and the entire world. We realize the nature of oneness, cause and effect. All fear, doubt, and suffering are gone.

The wish to share this clarity and realization arises naturally and spontaneously. Our entire life takes on new meaning. It is no longer about seeking wisdom and clarity for oneself, but for the sake of others, to assist them in reaching the same profound peace and freedom that we ourself have achieved. But this clarity itself becomes the second enemy. Pride rears it's ugly head, and we have what in Zen we refer to as "the stink of Zen."

2. Clarity

We have become attached to our realization and achievement, but we don't see it because we are so identified with our attainment we forget there was never anything to attain in the first place. We are now stuck in clarity, in being a realized person with knowledge and wisdom. This very clarity is holding us back from the third stage. We do not see that clarity comes and goes like everything else, impermanent and not fixed. We have made it into a thing and cling to it as if we can possess it as our own. We believe that we are clear and awakened, and superior to others who are not.

This becomes another place where the unhealthy and unaware ego comes into play. We now unintentionally speak to others in a patronizing and condescending way. We may say things like 'just let go' or 'just sit,' 'you are perfect, whole and complete as you are,' 'you are Buddha, just be it.'

It's as if we are on top of the mountain and most everyone else is in the mud down below. We may have become a guru, teacher, or leader of others, with something special to offer, even telling others to follow and submit completely to us.

Our attachment to clarity has become the problem and the enemy not only of ourselves but also of those who follow us. We believe we have something to share and to offer. But the road to hell is paved with good intentions. We have strayed far from where we first aspired to be. We may now have come to consider ourself a savior of all sentient beings.

3. Power

It is only when we completely let go of our attachment to clarity and realization that we embody the next stage in our evolution, which is becoming a person of power. A person with power has the capacity to empower others, not just teach, share or inspire, but actually empower them. It is as if by a touch, a wink, a word or a gesture we can turn others from not seeing to seeing, unrealized to realized, unawakened to awakened.

This capacity to empower others is a great gift and, at the same time, a great enemy. We may now become so identified with being a person of power that we see only its value and potential, ignoring how we abuse and misuse it. We are no longer a teacher. We have become a Master.

Our enemy now is power. We want to use it to change the world from delusion to enlightenment, from confusion to clarity, from unawakened to awakened, but we are unable to see our power trip or hear from others where we are abusing our power. It is as if we are drunk with our power and believe we are sober enough to drive. Others are afraid to confront us, they believe they should remain silent and acquiesce. This is of course the teaching that we adhere to and truly believe.

We now carry on our shoulders the very raft that brought us this far. To drop it, to forego the the transformations that this power now can facilitate in others, seems like insanity. Even if we realize that we are stuck on a power trip, to let go would be like leaping off a hundred foot cliff into the abyss — even if it's into the very river that will flow us to freedom — it's too frightening.

I don't know if we would ever make the leap if we had a choice. It takes such courage to let go of this power we have worked so hard to attain. It takes an exceptional person to do it voluntarily. We have become attached to being a person who can and 'should' empower and awaken others. It is only when we have no choice that we make the leap. We let go of our identity and mission as a savior and become what we always were, a human being. Now we can truly be touched by others and touch others' hearts and souls. Now we are approachable and real, truly alive, joyous and fulfilled.

4. Old age and death

We now face our fourth and final enemy: old age and death. We have come full circle. However, we have not lost our fearlessness;

now we are no longer afraid to face our fears and embody them. We have not lost our clarity; rather, we are no longer attached to it since we realize its transient nature. We have not lost our power to empower others; we are no longer attached to or identified with it.

Here we have the opportunity to face an enemy that we will never defeat. Whatever we do we will be beaten by life itself, and even surrendering to it doesn't work. Just as we learned along the Way, there is no answer. There is no escape, there is no way out. There is only this moment and the end of this moment.

We have realized that enlightenment and the absolute cannot be torn away from this relative existence and that they are truly one and inseparable, that whatever is born will face old age, decay and eventually death or the end.

There is tremendous joy and peace with the whole aging process. Life gets easier and simpler. We face this natural process with dignity and repose. There is no fear of death, life is just a constant process of relinquishment moment to moment. What comes next no one really knows and it all depends on forces of karma that we humans can't conceive.

We see is that we simply are human beings, subject to the same laws of nature and the universe as other living beings. I am not OK. You too are not OK, just human without the hope of ever really being perfect in a relative way. I'm not OK, you're not OK, but that's OK.

Here we live our life truly appreciating the subtle differences in people, not merely accepting that we are all different but really loving, enjoying and appreciating that you are not just like me, that we have different beliefs and ideologies, likes and dislikes, that you may be a republican and I a democrat, me a communist and you a capitalist, that our partner may prefer eating at home while I like eating out.

We have our preferences but we are not attached to them. Other people have their likes and dislikes, we treat them with love, respect, sensitivity and empathy. The differences are not just tolerated but loved.

V. The Path of the Human Being

Among the descriptions or maps of the Path in the Zen tradition, the one that I have found most illuminating and useful, both as a student and a teacher, is the Five Ranks of Master Tozan. This is a set of two poems by the great ninth century Chinese Master Tozan describing the interplay and integration of the Real, or Absolute Reality and the Apparent, or Relative Reality.

Each poem consists of five stanzas, which are used as koans, five from the perspective of the Real, and five from the perspective of the Apparent. Because his insights are so profound, and because he expressed them in poetic form, Tozan's Five Ranks has been translated and interpreted in many ways, including by many later great Zen Masters.

In my delineation of the stages, I have viewed each of them from the perspective of the Apex, rather than separately from the Apparent and the Real, as is normally done. Actually, the Path is not linear but more like smaller and greater spirals occurring throughout one's life, and all who undertake it have their own unique experiences, depending on their personal characteristics, gender and karma, their culture, historical moment and many other factors. My description is drawn from my own personal experiences, mixed with common and traditional representations of each stage, and may or may not exactly correspond to the experiences of others

1. The Shift: Glimpse of the Real, before a true awakening.

The first glimpse, or opening, can occur at any moment at any time in our life, either after years of practice or even prior to any conventional study. For me it happened in February 1971, before I even knew anything about Zen. It was, as it always is, unexpected and unpredictable. I glimpsed a reality different from the one I had been living in, which was a shocking experience, that turned my life around 180 degrees.

In Zen, the reality that we have been aware of up to this moment is called the apparent or relative reality, the world of form. The reality we have now glimpsed is called the real or absolute reality, the world of emptiness, of formless form. Although we may continue for many years to see them as two distinct realities, they are actually one. Form is no other than emptiness, emptiness no other than form. Form is exactly emptiness, emptiness exactly form. It is like the two sides of one coin.

Coming from our dualistic mind, this first opening of the non-dual can be anywhere from a glimpse to a very clear and powerful awakening. Sitting there in the Mojave Desert contemplating where is home, the personal self was dropped off, and I became one with the entire cosmos, God, the Creator and all creations, all things. I realized I was home, that I had never left, that wherever I am, I am always home.

This first awakening of the Bodhi Mind gave me new purpose, meaning and direction. Life seemed simple and uncomplicated, I felt liberated and at peace. I realized that I am the Way (the Tao) and the Path. It was like going sane, and seeing the way I had been perceiving life up to this moment — seeking fame, name and fortune — was insane.

What arose for me was a desire to continue to clarify the Way and to assist others in the process of awakening. This initial experience of Reality was so profoundly life-transforming that I felt compelled to share it with anyone willing to listen. It was like reading the greatest book or seeing the best movie ever made and just wanting to share it with everyone. It made me want to study everything about spirituality and psychology that I could get my hands on.

At this stage, after having had a glimpse of the Way, I was in the world but not yet really at peace with it, needing solitude deep in the mountains away from people and noisy city life. I tried to stay mindful and aware, sitting hours every day. I spent more than a year traveling and living alone deep in the mountains. Since I was not completely satisfied with my own clarity, I sought greater and deeper realizations of Reality.

This initial realization can differ in depth and clarity. It can be like a momentarily lit match in a pitch black room, or full daylight. We may even have many such awakenings, like earthquakes with aftershocks too numerous to count.

We have had a glimpse of our true nature, the Real, and have not yet integrated it into our daily life. It's like the shutter of a camera lens. It opens, giving us a clear experience of the Absolute, and then it closes again. We yearn for deeper and greater realizations of our true nature which has been recognized and is forever present but not yet fully realized or actualized.

2. Relinquishment: Surrender to the Real, the second stage prior to true awakening.

The first glimpse may occur after we have found our teacher or even before, it depends on our personal karma. In my case, until I met my root teacher I found more teachings in books and writings about the great traditions than I did in any living person. Either way we have begun to discard our false face, the contracted self that we call our identity, and long for our true face, our original self.

We eventually realize that if we want to further clarify the Way we need an external master to shape and direct us. This part of the journey is not something we can or should attempt on our own. I realized this spontaneously in March of '72 while I was still living as a hermit in the mountains near San Luis Obispo. Trying to be my own teacher would be like trying to do open heart surgery on myself. I knew that if I wanted to be a great athlete I would have to find a great coach. If I wanted to embody the Buddha's teaching I would have to place myself under the guidance of a living Buddha.

We may explore various teachings and practices and visit various masters before settling on our root teacher. Once we find him or her we may choose to completely surrender and submit, and begin the process of relinquishment. This was the decision I made in September of '72, more than a year and a half after my first opening, and the process which I described in the chapter on Submission.

It is a commitment to go through years of hard times giving up our deeply held beliefs, opinions, and concepts. It's hard enough to drop faulty or harmful ideas; even more difficult is letting go of the ones that seem precious, true, and of course right. It is like trying to go straight on a mountain path with ninety-nine switchbacks.

The training that many of us in my generation received, as I mentioned earlier, was patterned on a Japanese male monastic model. We had to be willing to be beaten (not necessarily with a stick or fist) and thrown into the fire of mind-stretching koans and scathing face-to-face meetings with the teacher, failing and being told again and again that we are wrong. In my case it also was being scolded for being too young and immature, too green and over-confident. There was even a time when my teacher told me that he hated me and did not trust me, which was absolutely devastating. This period of fourteen years was extremely difficult and painful for me, like being lifted up and then beaten down over and over again.

At this stage we keep falling back into deeply rooted patterns, to the Apparent reality. We are no longer the person we once were, but now who are we? The friends and most of the family I had before I began studying Zen were lost to me. Until then I was an athlete; overnight I became spiritual, working to deepen and clarify the experience of this first opening. This is where our focus is on the teacher, and it is here that we often mistake the finger for the moon, the teacher for the teaching.

If we persist, completely relinquish ourself to a living Buddha and are acknowledged as an awakened one, as the Buddha, eventually disappointment in our teacher and in our own realization and actualization can give rise to Great Doubt. Our projections are seen through, our illusions crumble, and we may become deeply disillusioned and disappointed. It was at this point — in March of '86, six years after receiving formal recognition as a Dharma successor and fourteen years after I began studying with him — that I realized my teacher with all his years of training and depth of realization was neither happy nor perfect, and neither was I. This sent me into Great Doubt.

When we look to and rely on one person as our teacher or

guru, that person may become our nightmare. This statement by Krishnamurti, which I read the day after realizing that my teacher was not happy, certainly contributed to my breaking through to the other side of Great Doubt, to Great Liberation. Until then I believed that teachers and masters were the higher authority and my role was always to surrender. It was as if I had put another head on my shoulders and become a two-headed freak. Now I had to face the terror that came up with this disappointment: If I could not depend on my master, who could I depend on? I began to doubt everyone and everything — the Buddha, all the great masters, even the great master Dogen.

3. Achievement: The Absolute Reality Attained, the stage of true awakening, dropped off body/mind.

All-encompassing doubt will eventually lead us to a great awakening. Sitting with Great Doubt we go through tremendous fear that we have no place or person to turn to. All hopes and expectations are dropped, and there is no one and nothing to lean or rely on. We are truly alone! It is here that the statement of the Buddha is realized, "I alone am the revered one."

A sudden, true awakening is an absence of experience, we have no words for it. It is completely different from all previous 'experiences.' Everything is gone, experience and experiencer. Just complete voidness, even a voidness of the void. This happened to me while I was sitting at the Kahala Hilton Hotel by the beach on Oahu in March of 1986.

The sky was blue, the ocean aqua, the clouds white, all was absolutely perfect with nothing lacking. As the great master Dogen said, the only thing that is realized is that the eyes are horizontal, nose is vertical, mountains are high, valleys low, the sun rises in the east and sets in the west. All doubt was gone and there was nothing attained nor to be attained, all was perfect, complete and whole just as it is.

True awakening is the realization that there is no Buddha, no Dharma, and no Way. Nothing is gained and no doubt remains.

We have faced our greatest enemy, the fear that there is no one and no thing that will save us. Body/mind is dropped off and there is a Great Death, and a Great Liberation. This is the absolute attained. There is no self and no other. This is the eternal now, free to come or to go, this is the stage of true grace.

For several months I felt no need to even communicate this to my teacher, Maezumi Roshi. There was no need for his approval. I had attained nothing. How could that be either approved or disapproved of? What could he confirm, that I had realized nothing, attained nothing, got nothing? This was the Truth. When I eventually did communicate what had happened, he approved it as a true enlightenment experience.

After this, one's life is never the same again, and certainly this was true for me. There is no higher authority, and yet there is tremendous love, gratitude, and appreciation for our teacher and all the masters that came before. There is no longer any gap between one's teacher and oneself. From here comes the expression, "I will never again doubt the great Zen Masters."

This is the summit, the realization that there is nothing to be attained and no place to go. There is no gate or window to pass through, it is a gateless gate, a windowless window. There is no karma and no cause and effect, they are absolutely one.

From here we inspire and encourage others to practice in order to realize complete freedom and liberation from suffering. Many may begin to follow and become students. We see them all as our children, to be encouraged and assisted to attain to the summit. We are more empowered to help and lead the way, since we have traveled the steep path all the way to the summit ourself.

This is how the third stage was for me, from '86 until June of '94, a little more than eight years. When we are teaching from the summit our voice has a very distinctive and recognizable tone. To the one on the mountaintop and the students and disciples down below it is inspired, indisputable, irresistible. To others, it may have a less positive ring. It is certainly different from the style of teaching that comes after descending the mountain. My own teaching, I think, illustrates the difference.

Twenty-two years ago, at the very end of this stage in 1993 and exactly half way along the journey that has brought me to the present moment, I published a book called *Beyond Sanity and Madness*. My intention in writing it was to express what I felt was necessary for the survival of Zen in the West. There was a sharpness in my tone at the current state of Zen practice. Nevertheless, it remains one of my favorite writings. It was, and is, a subject I feel passionate about and I wrote to challenge and inspire the reader, students as well as teachers, to practice in the true spirit of Zen. I believe it shows the power, as well as the power trip, that comes with being on top of the mountain:

> There are many people who encounter the Buddha-Dharma, but not all are receptive enough to hear the teaching with an open mind. Since doubt about the meaning of life is a driving force behind spiritual search, those who have gone through great loss or despair are usually more eager. It is easy, however, to lose this open-mindedness after some years of practice and become satisfied with a shallow understanding.
>
> If you have been practicing Zen for many years and have not yet penetrated to the essence of "the real Way is not difficult," you cannot even free yourself from a stone grave that is locked from the outside. How do you expect to liberate sentient beings? With your pitiful concerns about right and wrong, good and evil, you're not even worthy to be called a student of the Way, let alone a master of Zen! You should get yourself to a monastery and practice under a true master so you can swing your arms freely and move your legs without hindrance. You must be able to discern clearly the true Way from the false, Buddhas from deluded people.
>
> If you have not cut the root of dualistic mind completely, then you will go on transmigrating through the six realms and the three worlds eternally. You will be like a hungry ghost who is creeping around from here to there, searching for the Truth but unable to swallow it. Your belly will be unsatisfied, your thirst will be unquenchable, and your head will be filled with notions of right and wrong, good and evil. You will look to real masters with envy and jealousy and not know why you feel so miserable and vulnerable. It is only because you have not taken care of the great matter of life and death and still have uncertainty about who you are and where you are going.

If you really want to know what you are and where you come from, you must find an accomplished master to study with and go to the source of the matter, relinquishing everything that you have and becoming, truly, the person who stands alone on top of Mount Sumeru. Then you must drop to the very depths of hell where you walk freely with the homeless, begging for your food and accepting whatever pittance is offered to you.

Emperor Wu of Liang asked Bodhidharma, "What is the first principle of the holy teaching?" Bodhidharma said, "Vast emptiness, nothing holy." The Emperor said, "Who is this person confronting me?" Bodhidharma said, "I do not know." The emperor did not grasp his meaning. Bodhidharma then crossed the river and went on to the land of Wei.

Emperor Wu had not yet realized the primary principle of the true Dharma, so he had to ask the great Bodhidharma what it was. The Master, holding nothing back, revealed the Truth: "Vast emptiness. No holiness."

How do you understand this first principle of Zen? Do you understand it merely conceptually or have you become truly one with these words? Are you completely empty of yourself and no longer holy? Or are you still full of yourself and carrying the stink of Zen? Are you still seeking or have you really found?

If you have found anything whatsoever, even so much as a speck of dust, you are deluded and beyond help. If you are a young Zen novice, find yourself a good teacher and penetrate to the heart of this matter. If you are a senior Zen practitioner and still have doubt and uncertainty, take out Manjusri's sword and cut off your own head, or hand that sword to an accomplished swordsman and beg him to mercifully do the job for you. If you still see so much as a particle apart from yourself, you must cut off all discriminating thoughts.

We must mourn for the state of affairs of Zen today, for so few have truly realized Bodhidharma's profound meaning. How many can answer the question, "Why did Bodhidharma come from the West?" If you have any feeling of being special, holding on to any position or integrity, still having a shred of decency left, you cannot even save your own self.

You will be lost forever in the hell realm. Only after you have given up everything, even your pride and dignity, are you worthy to be called a true Zen monk. If you are still holding on to fame, name, position, or money, then you are still looking out from your prison window, trying to lead others to freedom. You haven't even so much as sniffed the fresh air of true liberation or smelled the sweet fragrance of the old barbarian!

At this point we have truly become the Way, there is no losing it after this. Wherever we tread is no other than the Path. We are completely free from all dualistic notions, free from dust and all delusions of self and other.

This is the time of greatness and silencing of tongues, this is the brilliant sun of enlightenment and no self, no karma and no others. Here there is no one superior and no head above our own. This is seeing eyeball to eyeball with all the great masters. This is the top of the mountain where the air is completely clear and visibility superb. There is absolutely no place higher to go. We have arrived, there is nothing lacking and absolutely no doubt remains.

When we are here, it appears there is nothing further to accomplish. The Apparent, relative reality seems unreal, an illusion from which we are finally liberated. In fact for some who hear about the need to descend the mountain, the very idea seems insane, as if one would be embracing delusion once again, back into a self with its fear, stress, anger, doubt and vulnerability. We may even believe this is the final stage of the Path.

Indeed, there are many spiritual practices based on this partial understanding of the Truth. It's a trap that I also fell into, which we call being stuck in the absolute. Here we may unconsciously get caught in ignoring the karmic law of cause and effect, simply because of the realization that they are one. We deny causation.

We are attached to our realization that we are limitless, without boundaries or borders. In fact the mention of boundaries may just anger us as psychological bullshit, merely concepts by which people bind themselves without so much as a rope. Many teachers and spiritual practices end here, without realizing that the descent is crucial if one wants to become truly human; many do not.

From this place no one, not even our own teacher, can tell us that we are stuck. In 1987 Maezumi Roshi tried. "Sensei," he said to me, "you are on a power trip." I couldn't really hear him for another seven years. Even then the stuckness doesn't just end; it continues on for years after this stage. Yasutani Roshi once told me he was stuck here for years. "As if I am no longer stuck here," he added, with a smile.

We are completely stuck in egohood, but we may not realize it for years. Believing we have reached Buddhahood, we still sit with a subtle wish to be truly egoless, because on some level we know that ego has returned, appropriated the experience, and made nothing into something.

Some have the capacity to realize they must cast away this state of nirvana, as Dogen Zenji says, raise the Bodhi Mind (the mind that seeks the Way), practice, realize, nirvana, cast it away, then raise the Bodhi Mind again, over and over. If we do realize that we are not truly free from ego, we may seek to cut off attachment to the self, to annihilate the ego.

However, if we wish to evolve to supreme awakening, no stage can be avoided or skipped. We will most likely become stuck here in egohood for some period. Over time an accumulation of karma may lead us to the fourth stage, the great descent, Advanced Achievement.

Maybe some great beings can move quickly through these inevitable stages, but only the ego believes it can avoid or leap past one or more of them. Maybe with guidance from someone who has gone through them we can actually move through these phases more quickly and stay stuck for a shorter time, and therefore create less harm.

4. Advanced Achievement: The great descent, the relative attained, the first stage post-true enlightenment.

Having spent years on top of the mountain in a state of grace free from suffering, fear and distress, we experience the next stage of the Way, Advanced Achievement. This is when we descend from the summit, dropping our wish to be egoless and our attachment to our enlightenment.

It began for me during a series of retreats in Europe, June of

1994, as I was doing an advanced practice to annihilate my ego. While leading a retreat in the Netherlands I had what I describe as a great fall and ended up quite dysfunctional, like a puddle on the floor, for two consecutive nights. Like Humpty Dumpty my ego was shattered into hundreds of pieces and it took a year or more to put it back together again. However, since then it has never been so solid, fixed or substantial as it was before this great fall.

All human emotions, all kinds of suffering are back, but in a completely different way than before. One has completely returned to the relative world but without walls or barriers. Here one experiences one's vulnerability and mortality. This is the stage represented by the circle, or *enso*, in the ninth of the Ten Oxherding pictures.

At first one may attempt to ascend the mountain once again, but now the mountain is like sheer ice and cannot be climbed, there is no place to get a grip. Over time one comes to terms with the reality that there is truly no way back and it is completely futile to continue to attempt to ascend. As long as one is trying to return to the summit it is a less mature phase of the Fourth Rank.

This is the first descent of the mountain, which may not occur before we have spent years enjoying the beautiful view from the summit. Back in the Apparent, relative world, there is once again you and me, self and others, fear and fearlessness. The relative and the absolute are like two crossed swords, there is no need for either one to withdraw or to dominate the other. The absolute is no longer the only truth, it is just one of two sides of the Truth. In fact at this stage the absolute is seen as an escape from the relative reality of fear and suffering. This is the beginning of the integration of the personal and the impersonal, the relative and the absolute, the Apparent and the Real.

Mountains are once again mountains, rivers once again rivers. We have returned to the world of difference, the apparent world where we know that we are all equal and yet no two are the same and all are absolutely unique. True appreciation for differences arises without judgements.

Here we see the truth of the saying that the difference between an enlightened person and an ordinary person is that the enlightened person knows there is no difference while the ordinary person believes there is.

Having descended — or more accurately, fallen — from the absolute or enlightened stage, one may with time and further practice become a master, not just of how to ascend the mountain but also how to also descend and work with the relative reality and our shadows.

Here one gains the power to empower others by being with them where they are and assisting them to ascend the mountain rather than speaking down to them from above. This is Kanzeon Bodhisattva who can manifest in many different forms, appear in different times and places freely without restriction to liberate people of all walks of life, from the lowest to the highest.

Reaching what seems like the very bottom, one is truly a soaring spirit, empowered to awaken all beings with whom one comes into contact, and many may be awakened by a touch, a glance, a word or a gesture. Here Buddhas and sentient beings are co-existing with neither hindering the other, Buddhas awakening ordinary beings to deeper awareness and accomplishment. Opposites are transcended and seen clearly from the Apex for what they are: suchness, Tathagata, Buddha attained. Here one becomes identified as a Buddha that gives birth to Buddhas, Mahavairochana Buddha, the parent of all Buddhas.

In this fourth stage, we may get caught by the power to empower, as I did, and become inflated and arrogant about our abilities to awaken others. This stage can last decades. We may empower hundreds or even thousands and change lives forever. The power to empower others gives us a sense of greatness as Kanzeon Bodhisattva or as Mahavairochana Buddha.

Until this moment we may have experienced, even several times, the rug being pulled out from under us, but haven't a clue that the sky can still fall, as Trungpa Rinpoche once said, like a giant pancake on our head. I believed I had completely descended the mountain. It wasn't until January of 2011 that the sky fell on my head and I descended to the very bottom, all the way down to sea level.

5. *Absolute Achievement: Unity Attained, the second stage post-true enlightenment, the mature Apex.*

Absolute Achievement is reached only by a second descent of the mountain. The earlier one, the Fourth Rank, turns out to have been only partial. Now we see we had landed on a magnificent plateau, called Buddha-Dharma, and there is still further to fall. We can see that the fourth stage had at least two phases, a less mature and a more mature. The second was a period of building up a capacity and ability to empower. Our great confidence and faith were projected outward, and were met with projections of greatness.

In this fifth stage we lose everything. It is a new death, only more complete than anything previously experienced, a death of everything that we are identified as, of our whole identity. Here we are like a phoenix rising from the ashes. We project nothing special, and the projections of others are also gone. It is a loss not just of Buddha-Dharma but of position, status and identity, a loss of both man and ox. There is absolutely nothing to seek nor any place to go. We have become a person of no rank or position, a true human being.

This is the identity of relative and absolute attained, where the Apparent world and the Real are no longer seen as two separate realities. With the absence of projections from others and no longer being seen as great, enlightened or special, we once again are completely ordinary. We have arrived at neither being nor non-being, and yet beyond both being and non-being, where few dare to go of their own volition, transcending and embracing both the relational as well as the non-relational.

Now we can see ourself and our shadows more clearly, and there is an absence of any supposed attainment. The quest for Buddhahood appears truly shameful, a fool's folly. The path is no longer seen as a journey but a trip. Realizing without a shadow of doubt that no one has attained anything, for it is forever unattainable and there is no self to attain it, we can fully appreciate the statement, "I don't say there is no Zen, only no masters of Zen."

We become a beginner once again, a follower of the Way. This is unity attained and integration continues endlessly. It is completely ordinary and yet not ordinary at all. We are no longer attached to either praise or blame, affirmation or negation, winning or losing. We project a calm, happy and joyous mind. It is unnecessary to journey to visit sages or masters. It is full circle back to where we started, and yet not. All is seen as a big detour, and yet quite a journey.

Having truly left one's everyday life many decades ago, having gained nothing, having lost everything, one returns home to sit amongst the coals and ashes of one's own life. Like a lotus in muddy water, one lives amongst the people, unrecognized by many, a hazy moon, sometimes brilliantly shining sometimes unnoticed. This is returning to the marketplace with gift-bestowing hands, a bag of goodies over one's shoulder and a jug of wine in one's hand.

One has come full circle and yet not necessarily finished, since it is continuous spiral of practice and constant refinement. The yearning here is to fade into the woodwork and live completely ordinary, wiping off the dust of the world, mingling with ordinary people. No trace of enlightenment remains and this no trace goes on endlessly. One has ascended peak after peak and descended into numerous valleys, following the streams and sitting beside the great oceans.

Looking back one sits serenely in a silk-like samadhi for hours doing absolutely nothing. All seeking has ceased and yet there is a continuous refinement of one's life. Wherever one goes people in all walks of life are touched. How beautiful, one thinks, it is to do nothing, and then to rest afterwards.

13

What I Mean by Zen Practice

Zen practice is often described as a journey; it could also be seen as one big trip or detour, since we seem to go to such great lengths just to arrive back home. When we first set out we want to discover something more than our selves. In all my years of practice I could neither find nor get rid of my "self." Wherever I went there "I" was. If I had found more it would have been like putting another head on my shoulders. In the end all I found was "me." The difference is that now I am at peace with myself, free and truly happy.

Our journey is inward. To deepen and clarify the Way we take time to sit quietly alone or together with others. In our sitting we don't make distinctions between real and unreal or try to shut out the world. We cease having preferences or distinguishing between desirable and undesirable, right and wrong, good and bad, self and other, insane and sane.

We hold no preference for or against anything that arises. If there is a right way to sit then there is going to be a wrong way, and as human beings we will find the wrong way. If there is a good way then there will be a bad way, etc. We don't try to make our mind blank or quiet; we simply sit allowing whatever arises to arise and just letting it go as it goes, seeing all things as empty and without substance, like bubbles rising to the surface of the water. We sit without a goal or aim, embracing both thinking and not-thinking, seeking and not-seeking, awake or asleep, conscious or unconscious, attentive or inattentive.

"What is true meditation?" Hakuin wrote. "It is to make everything: coughing, swallowing, waving the arms, motion, stillness, words, action, the evil and good, prosperity and shame, gain and loss, right and wrong, into one single koan."

Life is paradox, full of polarities that seem irreconcilable. Within ourselves and in the world at large — politically, religiously, economically and socially — the forces of opposition may never have been more polarized. We need to look at how we deal with this polarization both externally and internally. We need to discover how to embrace and transcend the polarities of life without being attached to a particular position or identified with a particular view, to live with the awareness that it is all views, and whether a particular view is right or wrong just depends on where one is standing.

Even the view I'm advancing here is just another view. No matter how complete or encompassing it may be, still it's just another perspective. Even though I may consider it better or more beneficial or wise than other views, I need to be aware that the moment I express it, that is a place I where I may be stuck.

This particular view may be more inclusive than others but it is still just a perspective. When we take a particular view as the only right or correct one we limit and diminish ourselves. No matter how great or profound our view or belief, as soon as we get stuck in it, we have made our way or understanding right and others wrong.

The way of embracing both seemingly opposing views simultaneously without attachment to either is what I call coming from the Apex. Imagine a triangle with the corners of the base of the triangle being two seeming opposites, a dualistic view and a non-dual view, for example thinking and not-thinking. The Apex is beyond thinking and not-thinking, we can call it non-thinking. It includes both thinking and not-thinking and yet transcends them. When the thinking mind is fully owned, embodied and empowered, we realize that thinking is truly not-thinking. When the opposites are both owned, we see they are not really opposite but one and the same. When both are embodied and empowered, that is the Apex functioning freely.

The challenge facing each of us today and our entire world is how to embody and live this Apex perspective. But even in Buddhism and in Zen this polarization persists. As the author of *The Gateless Gate* warned centuries ago, there are those of us who tie ourselves up without a rope, trying so hard to follow rules and regulations and being politically correct, while others act freely without restraint, behaving like heretics.

Or we get caught up in opposing the spiritual and the psychological, as if seeing the value in one makes the other wrong. We in Zen, and Buddhists in general, often put therapy down; psychotherapists often disparage spiritual experiences, particularly awakening to no-ego or no-mind, as spiritual bypassing or even dangerous practices. It's true we can use the transcendent to escape from our life or the experience of no-ego to disown or deny the ego, but these pitfalls have long been recognized within the Zen tradition, and do not invalidate its insights and wisdom.

We might think that as Zen practitioners we'd have gotten past this kind of polarization. Easier said than done. We can become aware of an Apex perspective and still not be able to actualize it in our life. So many of us preach love and compassion all the while judging and condemning others for what we see as their imperfections. There is always a gap between our realization or insight and actualizing or embodying it in our daily lives. This is where practices such as zazen and others help integrate these awarenesses into our life.

The gap between realization and actualization *is* practice. Realizations always come suddenly while actualizing and integrating our insights simply takes time. The historical Buddha was quite clear about this. He offered these eight practices, eight awareness for living an awakened life: have few desires, know how to be satisfied with the way it is, live with serenity, be diligent and persevere, be mindful and aware, practice samadhi, practice wisdom, and avoid idle talk.

We can have a state experience of transcending the self, but to live and embody non-attachment to self is not so easy. Similarly, a state experience of the Apex is not so difficult to achieve, but to truly live and embody the extremes without being attached to them or acting them out is not so easy. It is easy to fall into one extreme or other, to be, for example, too identified with the personal self and remain in suffering and fear, or to go the other extreme and get stuck in the impersonal and be absent in relationships. But the Apex is not a fixed place or position; on the contrary, because it is not fixed or stuck it can hold the tension of opposites and respond appropriately moment by moment.

So the challenge for us is, how do we manifest the Apex and allow it to evolve? How do we live moment to moment without being stuck in any particular voice or state but flowing freely from voice to voice without hindrance, dynamically, full of juice and aliveness, aligned with wisdom and compassion? This is what I mean by Zen practice.

BIG MIND EVOLVES

14

Exploring the Self with Big Mind

To explore the Buddha Way is to explore the self. To explore the self
is to drop the self. To drop the self is to be actualized by the ten thousand dharmas [all phenomena]. When actualized by the ten thousand
dharmas, body and mind as well as the bodies and minds of others
drop off. With time and further deepening no trace of enlightenment
remains, and this no-trace continues endlessly.

— Dogen Zenji, *Genjokoan*

A Bodhisattva does not cling to the idea of ego entity, of a being, or
of a separate self.

— The Buddha, *The Diamond Sutra*

These two well-known statements point to what may seem to
our logical mind a paradox at the heart of Buddhist teachings. The
self? What self? For some who have realized no self the "self" is just
an idea, an illusion that doesn't exist. How can we explore it? And
why should we? Big Mind offers one way to experience the truth
that both the Buddha and Master Dogen wanted us to realize.

What did Dogen Zenji mean by 'to explore the Buddha Way is
to explore the self'? I don't know how it is in the East, but here in
the West many of us want to skip this step in our Zen practice, or
believe it is an irrelevant detour on the way to the experience of great
enlightenment. We also think Dogen Zenji was describing some
kind of linear step-by-step program rather than a process in which
these actions occur simultaneously and continuously. Moment by
moment we are exploring the self as we are dropping the self as we
are being actualized by the ten thousand dharmas.

To explore the self really means to explore all aspects of the self
and to realize their essential nature as empty and void of substance
and yet Buddha-Dharma. Each aspect of self is Buddha, perfect,

complete and whole as it is when truly acknowledged, owned and embodied for what it is, Dharma. When we realize this we can let go of identifying with the self and see it for what it is, a concept or notion and yet Dharma, since all phenomena (dharmas), including our ephemeral concepts, are Dharma. When we see the self for what it is we realize that the self is actualized by the ten thousand dharmas, they are not separate and yet not one either.

In facilitating the Big Mind process, in my own meditation or with others, I often ask that we separate and distance ourself from "the self." This doesn't make sense to the logical mind, and yet we can do it. When we do, it becomes easier to let go of the idea of an ego entity or a separate self, to see through the illusion of self and to drop it. And this allows us to clearly see and get in touch with particular aspects of the self — states of mind — often for the first time.

Here is an example of something I realized a couple of years ago, that has helped me in my understanding and may be helpful to others: I was working with the voice of "the one who is innocent." Using the Big Mind process, naming and invoking it as a separate aspect of the self and identifying with it rather than with the self, I was able to see clearly that as the voice of the one who is innocent I am innocent, but he, the so-called "self," is in no way innocent. What self is? No one is innocent; only the voice the one who is innocent is innocent.

I also realized that this voice was extremely disowned within me, and maybe in most of us. To be able to declare as this voice that I am completely innocent is most likely the only way any of us can say so, because of course none of us is completely innocent, maybe even since birth. The moment this voice declares "I am innocent," it can clearly see — without blame, shame or defensiveness — that the self is not innocent.

That allows the "self" to take responsibility for what it is guilty of and it's hurtful behavior or actions. The opposite is also just as true. If I speak as the voice of the one who is guilty, then I can clearly see that the "self," Genpo, is not the one who is guilty. It is me, the voice of the one who is not so innocent, that is guilty. Rather than denying or ignoring our guilt, owning this voice allows us to take full responsibility for our karma, for cause and effect. When we embody and empower a voice, the self is seen more clearly for what it is. We are then able to realize that to cling to the idea of an ego as a solid, separate, fixed self or being, is delusion.

The self can now take full responsibility for its actions and reactions and the karma that it has created. Only this particular voice, this aspect of the self, is innocent or guilty, not the self. To separate the voice from the self is a crucial point, and very subtle. It is one of the skillful means for transmitting the teachings that the Big Mind process offers us.

Now we can ask to speak to "the opposite of the one who is innocent." From here I can own that I am not innocent; only that other voice, of "the one who is innocent" is innocent, not Genpo. I no longer need to defend or explain my lack of innocence or guilt. I am not innocent at all; I am guilty of all kinds of things that I can now acknowledge, own and take responsibility for, how I have harmed and hurt others. Again, it is essential to see that I am not speaking as the self, I am "the opposite of the one who is innocent."

From here I can then fully own the Apex, where I am simultaneously and completely both innocent and not innocent. I am both innocent and guilty as well as neither innocent nor guilty. *Neti neti*, not this, not that either, and not not that. From here I do not have to plead my innocence or be stuck in feeling bad or guilty for what I have done. I no longer need to make excuses or be a victim, nor resent or ignore cause and effect.

I am never innocent nor am I ever just guilty either. There is always one who is innocent and one who is not innocent too. I know I am responsible for my actions and reactions, for the karma I have created and will continue to create, for responding with wisdom and compassion in whatever situation arises in my life.

15

What Big Mind Has Brought to Zen Practice

Each and every aspect of the self — or voice, as I refer to them — can function either in a mature and healthy fashion that enhances our life or, when it is unhealthy and immature, in a way that sabotages our whole system. The Big Mind process allows us to recognize and awaken these various aspects of ourselves, to own and appreciate them, and thereby empower them to manifest in our life aligned with wisdom and compassion.

The Controller, for example, the voice that controls which other voices are permitted to speak, when disowned, is closely aligned with fear, and will only grant permission for a particular voice to come out if it feels safe. The voice itself has to feel that you, the one truly in charge, loves, appreciates, honors and respects it, and that you own, embody, and empower it to do its job. Then it becomes like putty in your hands, and will work for you rather than against you. When the Controller is awakened and really working for you, it transforms into the Master, and is no longer operating out of fear, but out of wisdom, love and compassion.

Every voice that is out there in the world, the entire range from the positive to the seemingly negative, is within every one of us. The voice of the Buddha, God, Universal Consciousness, the great sages — are all within us. Imagine the worst possible voice out there. We don't want to acknowledge that it too is within us. And yet each voice, when we allow it to speak, to be acknowledged, owned, empowered and mature, will offer us something of great value.

Every voice when disowned and buried, will come out covertly and may actually work against us. We tend to see particular voices as undesirable and unacceptable, even repulsive or evil, because we associate them with how they manifest, in others or in ourselves, when they are disowned and unawakened, and therefore hate with a vengeance admitting they are within us. But if we don't acknowledge them, they come out in perverted thoughts or actions. As long as a voice is disowned and immature, buried, down in the basement, it doesn't have vision, it doesn't have light, it can come out in harmful and negative ways.

What we are talking about here is energy: in its negative form it is destructive, if we can flip it from negative to positive it works for us. Every negative voice, when you flip it, transcends and includes itself. This means it goes beyond itself and is no longer recognizable by its old name.

Fear when awakened can become wakefulness, attentiveness, awareness. Anger can become ruthless compassion. Powerlessness can become surrender and liberation, unworthiness flip into great appreciation and gratitude. Every voice will transcend itself, move beyond its label.

It is because we get to know these aspects in their immature, negative state that we label them that way. "Ego" has a negative connotation, whereas Ego is just awareness of self which gives us our sense of a continuing identity. Coming from an Awakened Ego means coming from a healthy and mature place, a place that is there to serve the self, to assist the self to function well in society.

You don't need to fear any voice. What you want to do is get to know that voice, to acknowledge it, learn about it, own and embody it, and eventually even empower it to do its job. Fear is here to protect you, and when flipped to positive it becomes awareness, attentiveness, wakefulness. Ego is here to help you to be aware and responsible in dealing with the world, to know your healthy boundaries.

We need not fear going into these dark and scary places within us and befriending these seemingly negative voices. By giving them voice, by owning and embodying them we empower them to actually serve us in a healthy and mature way.

Now traditional Zen wasn't particularly aware of or interested in these voices, so what we did was suppress them, push them down to gain control. The Buddha said that one who masters his own mind is like a warrior who defeats ten thousand enemies in battle singlehandedly. It's true, but it's much better to do it with love and compassion than to suppress, because what we have learned through Western psychotherapy and the Big Mind/Big Heart process is that every voice loves to be asked rather than told. Just like a child. You tell your child, 'Don't do that!' — you know they're going to do it. You say, 'Please don't do that, it's going to be hurtful,' most likely if they have any wisdom at all, they're going to obey.

People are the same way. You try to suppress people, they're going to rebel. Ask them lovingly, kindly, 'I need your help, your support,' almost everybody is going to jump in and say, 'Yes, absolutely, I'm happy to support you.' The voices are the same, because each one is human-like, a being.

So the key to the Big Mind work is asking for permission rather than ordering or suppressing. The more you suppress a voice, the more it cries out for attention. You take the Thinking Mind and you try to suppress it, to make it shut up, it doesn't work. It just becomes more active. You say to the Thinking Mind, 'You know I love and appreciate you and I want you to just think all you want,' and it goes 'Uhhh,' — it just goes stupid, it goes quiet, unless there's a reason to think about something. Then it will come forth with thinking. But it doesn't really have much to say if there's not an appropriate time and place for it. It just lays still, like a kitty or a doggie, until it's time, and then it comes out.

This, I feel, is a useful and powerful method for transmitting the teachings that the Big Mind process has brought to Zen practice. Every voice, like every being is aspiring to full awakening, to full consciousness. Every voice aspires to be recognized and embraced, loved and respected. We're all growing. Trees grow, plants grow, everything is aspiring to grow. Once we stop growing physically, the only ways left are in consciousness and awareness, heart and relatedness, and these may be the only kind of growth that's endless.

16

The Buddhist Roots of the Big Mind Process

Ever since I first discovered the Big Mind process and began using it in my teaching in 1999, there have been some people who questioned not only its effectiveness but whether it could really be considered a Zen Buddhist practice. I think time has settled, and will continue to answer the first question. As for the second, I have always known that Big Mind was rooted in my own training and understanding of the teachings and the tradition, and also believed that it is firmly rooted in historical Buddhist teachings and practices.

I am not a scholar, but I am fortunate to have a Buddhist scholar among my successors. Maurice Shonen Knegtel Sensei teaches Buddhist philosophy at universities in The Netherlands and Belgium and has published several books on Buddhism and contemporary spirituality. He has written a perceptive article [1] about the Buddhist roots of the Big Mind process the substance of which I reproduce here.

The historical Buddha served as a spiritual midwife to his students, much as his contemporary, Socrates, did in our Western culture. Both were helping students give birth to their own insights, rather than teaching them about something they had not experienced themselves. In Zen, masters use various skillful means such as 'turning words' to do exactly the same thing. These are like fingers pointing at the moon, not to be mistaken for the moon itself. The Big Mind process is one such skillful means, with roots deep in Buddhist teachings that go back to the historical Buddha himself:

---

[1] *The Wonder of Teaching: The Big Mind process in a Buddhist perspective,* Maurice Shonen Knegtel Sensei, http://bigmind.org/blog/the-wonder-of-teaching.

A student named Vaccha asked Gautama the Buddha: "Is there any view which you have adopted, Gautama?"

"The adoption of views is a term discarded for the truth-finder, who has had actual vision of the nature, origin and cessation of things material, of feelings, of perception, of deeply rooted patterns, and of consciousness. Therefore it is that, by destroying, stilling, suppressing, discarding and renouncing all supposing, all imaginings, and all tendencies to the pride of saying I or mine, the truth-finder is delivered because no fuel is left to keep such things going."

"When his heart is thus delivered, Gautama, where is an almsman reborn hereafter?"

"Reborn does not apply to him."

"Then he is not reborn?"

"Not-reborn does not apply."

"Then he is both reborn and not reborn?"

"Reborn and not-reborn does not apply."

"Then he is neither reborn nor not reborn?"

"Neither reborn nor not-reborn does not apply to him."

"To each and all of my questions, Gautama, you have replied in the negative. I am at a loss and bewildered, the measure of confidence you inspired by your former talk has disappeared."

After bringing the student to the point of realizing he cannot grasp the ungraspable with his concepts and logic, the Buddha leads him to a completely different perspective:

"You ought to be at a loss and bewildered, Vaccha. For this doctrine is profound, recondite, hard to comprehend, excellent, beyond dialectic, subtle, only to be understood by the wise. To you it is difficult, who hold other views and belong to another faith and objective [...]. So I in turn will question you, for such answer as you see fit to give. What think you, Vaccha? If there were a blaze in front of you, would you know it?"

"Yes."

"If you were asked what made that fire blaze, could you give an answer?"

"I should answer that what made it blaze, was the fuel. [...]"

"If the fire went out, would you know it had gone out?"

"Yes."

"If now you were asked in what direction the fire had gone, whether to the east, west, north or south, could you give an answer?"

"The answer does not apply. [...]"

The student finally 'gets' it, and his reaction recalls the surprise and gratitude of Zen students in many stories and koans centuries later:

> "Magnificent, Master Gautama! Magnificent, Master Gautama! You have made the Dharma clear in many ways, as though you were turning upright what had been overthrown, revealing what was hidden, showing the way to one who was lost, or holding up a lamp in the dark for those with eyesight to see forms. [...]"[2]

The Buddha has guided his student not by preaching or explaining but by enabling him to see for himself that the truth-finder is "neither reborn nor not-reborn," and is indeed not separate from himself.

BIG MIND AND ABHIDHARMA

The Big Mind process works the same way. The facilitator seldom talks *about* the Dharma; but rather guides students to a place where they themselves express the Dharma. They just agree to allow the facilitator to speak to aspects of themselves that may as yet be unawakened, the voice of wisdom, or compassion, or non-seeking mind, or Big Mind, which is in fact the voice of the awakened one. In this way they immediately access states of mind they were seeking all their lives, but not by means of the familiar route of dualistic thinking.

Zen has always been called the Sudden School of awakening. Each of us is already intrinsically awake but just hasn't realized it yet. So the realization is sudden, it takes no time. Of course actualizing it in our daily life does take time.

Referring to different aspects of mind as 'voices' is a contemporary, Western way (derived from the Voice Dialogue work of Drs. Hal and Sidra Stone) of speaking of Buddhist *dharmas*. In the Abhidharma, which means 'the Higher Dharma,' we find lists of all these aspects of mind. Among them are sense organs and sense objects, birth, death, impermanence, doubt and ignorance, but also emotions like hatred, pride and anger.

---

[2] *Majjhima Nikaya*, translated by Robert Chalmers, Oxford University Press, London, 1926, Vol. I, pp. 342-344.

In the early Abhidharma traditions in fourth century B.C. India, dharmas were considered as 'events' or 'items of experience.'[3] They are non-substantial manifestations of the Dharma, which exist in dependent co-arising with all other non-substantial manifestations, like images in a mirror. All the dharmas listed in the Abhidharma texts refer back to items of experience named by the Buddha himself in his teachings, and Buddhist monks and nuns used them for meditation.

Much later, in the fourth century A.D., the dharmas were considered aspects of mind by the 'Mind-only' (Yogacara) school of Mahayana Buddhism. The Big Mind process is a Western expression of the Yogacara teaching that everything is Mind. And the meditation of the Yogacarins on the dharmas is experienced in a Buddhist/Jungian process in which one awakens and owns an aspect of mind by giving voice to it.

It is no wonder that the Big Mind process is in tune with the Yogacara teaching of Mind-only. When Chan (Zen) appeared in China in the seventh century A.D., as the fruit of a long and highly complicated process of assimilation of Indian Buddhism with Chinese Taoism and Confucianism, it was called the Lankavatara School, named after the Sutra that formed the basis of the Yogacarin teaching.

This Sutra's crucial influence is emphasized in Zen tradition by the legend that when Bodhidharma brought Zen from India to China, he carried only one book with him in his travels, the Lankavatara Sutra. Early great Chan Masters like Baso emphasized Mind in the same way the Yogacarins did, and often referred to the Lankavatara Sutra.

In a famous koan when Zen Master Baso was asked, "What is Buddha?" he answered, "Mind is Buddha." The student had a deep realization. At another time when he was asked, "What is Buddha?" Baso answered, "No mind no Buddha."

---

[3] *History of Buddhist Philosophy*, David Kalupahana, University of Hawaii Press, Honolulu, 1992, p. 145.

Big Mind, Koan and Tathagathagarba (Buddha Matrix)

Both the Big Mind process and koan practice depend on the teacher's trust that the student can access the enlightened state of mind. In koan practice the student is asked to be one with the enlightened mind of the master and the koan itself. In the Big Mind process the student may be asked to be one with an aspect of mind, or a koan, or even with the master. Aspects or states of mind that can be facilitated and explored are virtually unlimited.

The experience of being one with whatever is asked for is so much easier in the Big Mind process than in koan training because the facilitator is just asking to speak to a voice, and the student responds without effort, becomes one with that aspect of mind and gives voice to it.

Koan training can involve a lot of thinking, and often a stressful effort to identify with the mind of the master or to be one with the koan. In the playfulness of the Big Mind process oneness happens effortlessly because of the trust or faith in the master or facilitator. No effort or dualistic thinking is required; in fact it is simply bypassed. This non-effort is the key to the effectiveness of the process.

Of course it can be a struggle to speak from a disowned voice, unless one is guided by a skilled facilitator. However, these disowned voices can be the most interesting to explore, because they are the very ones that keep us stuck and unable to live as integrating free-functioning human beings.

The real juice of our life is in these disowned voices or aspects of self. They include the many facets of suffering which some modern day practices do not really address, but which, as Buddha taught, cannot be escaped and must be faced and become one with. Awakening them enables us, in Master Rinzai's words, to 'remove barriers and undo knots.' Owning them makes our lives richer, more joyful, more interesting, more refined.

Both koan training and the Big Mind process are rooted in the third century A.D. Indian teaching of the Tathagathagarba, which is one of the three most fundamental tenets of Mahayana Buddhism, the other two being the identity of form and emptiness, and the figure of the Bodhisattva. Tathagathagarba — 'the womb of the Buddha,' or 'the Buddha Matrix' — states that everything is Buddha-nature.

If you trust this, your life is the life of the Buddha. This faith or trust makes it is possible to be one with the mind of an enlightened master when working on a koan, and it enables participants in the Big Mind process to respond when the facilitator asks 'whom I speaking to?' with 'I am Wisdom,' or 'I am Compassion,' or 'I am Big Mind.' Students can see for themselves that they are all-inclusive, unborn and therefore undying.

Zen Master Bankei said, "Just have faith that the Unborn Buddha Mind is functioning perfectly right here and now," without beginning or end, one with everything and everybody. But who can say 'right here and now I am the Awakened One'?

That is the experience the Big Mind process makes possible. To fully trust and integrate this insight takes time. Still, the fact that it is possible to speak to the Enlightened One right now, as we do in both koan practice and the Big Mind process, substantiates this most fundamental Mahayana teaching of the Tathagathagarba.

The Big Mind process, where we freely and playfully invoke aspects of mind often referred to as voices, which can tell us a great deal about themselves, and about ourselves, is a direct descendant of the methods of these early Chinese masters.

We find it in many Zen stories, for example when Master Dogo sees Master Ungan sweeping the Temple yard and says, "I see you're hard at it!" and Ungan replies, "Old man you should know the one who is not hard it!" And in the great Master Zuigan who would hike to the top of the mountain behind his monastery as his daily practice. Sitting in zazen he asked himself out loud, "Master are you in?" "Yes!" he answered himself. "Are you awake?" "Yes!" "Don't be deceived!" "No I won't!"

Big Mind and Early Chan

The evolution of Chan in seventh century A.D. China suggests how Buddhism will develop in the West. If it is to take root in our culture and society, it will be so thoroughly transformed that a Japanese, Tibetan or Thai Buddhist might not recognize it as Buddhism. Even its name could change. Chan was a truly Chinese form of Indian Mahayana Buddhism. Neither the name Chan, nor the way of teaching, nor the practices existed before the seventh century A.D.

The same is true for Big Mind/Big Heart. It is a genuine Western form of Zen Buddhism, with a Western name, a Western way of teaching based on Zen realization and Voice Dialogue, and a Western mode of practice, seated in chairs and guided by a facilitator. Nevertheless, this Western form is totally in tune with traditional Buddhist teaching. The way the facilitator works with students goes back to the way the Buddha worked with his disciples. The concept of Big Mind and the voices that are worked with go back to the Yogacara School's concept of Mind-only and the dharmas in the Abhidharma traditions. And the teaching of the Tathagathagarba accounts for why it is not heretical to speak directly to the voice of the Awakened One. Big Mind/Big Heart Zen is certainly a crucial part of the Fourth Turning of Buddhism.

There is another thing we can learn from the development of early Chan in China. During the first two centuries of its development in the classical period of Chan, the source of so many memorable stories of encounters between Master and student, the teaching was brought to life through what is called 'the methodless method.'

Teaching happened spontaneously, using whatever was at hand in the moment. Take for example the following dialogue, in which Master Baso and his student Hyakujo Ekai are walking in the mountains:

> A flock of wild ducks flew past them.
> Baso said: "What's that?"
> Hyakujo said: "Wild ducks."

Baso said: "Where'd they go?"
Hyakujo said: "They flew away."
Baso twisted Hyakujo's nose so hard he cried out.
Baso said: "So you say they've flown away!"
Hearing these words Hyakujo attained enlightenment.

We don't know exactly how they practiced in those early ages of Chan. What we do know is that the Masters and their students often subsisted by working long days in the fields. Undoubtedly, Masters were regarded with the respect, even reverence, characteristic of traditional Chinese culture, their spoken and recorded teachings treasured and handed down by their students and successors. However, it's remarkable how accounts of their teaching, particularly in the numerous koan collections, reflect the way teaching, practice and realization occurred in everyday activity, like farming, walking through the mountains, drinking tea, cleaning, or just talking. Probably they did not sit that much in formal zazen, and the early Masters rarely talk about sitting practice.

Zen was not yet formalized with rituals and ceremonial practices, as it was later in Sung China (tenth to fourteenth century A.D.), Korea, Vietnam and Japan. Early Chan was a living religion, not dependent on formal Dharma talks by teachers and formal sitting or interviews between teacher and student. Enlightenment was found and expressed in daily activities. And the old Masters' way of enabling students to embody and express the Dharma was essentially the same as the historical Buddha's.

The Big Mind process offers the same living Zen in a contemporary vehicle, a playful game of giving voice to whatever dharma is coming up, skillfully practicing the same 'methodless method' the Buddha and early Chan Masters used. Naturally this way of teaching looks different from the way we picture the Chinese a millennium later, and is perhaps as far removed from it as they were from their Buddhist ancestors yet another millennium earlier.

The living spirit of Zen has always adapted to changing times and places. If there is one thing our present day and age sorely needs, it is ways to help us connect with this living spirituality. One such way is Big Mind / Big Heart.

17

Big Heart Zen and Psychotherapy

Of course there are many fundamental differences between Western psychotherapy and Zen. One of the biggest is their starting point. In Buddha's understanding, which came directly out of his enlightenment, all sentient beings are complete, whole and perfect as they are, just as every tree, plant or animal is perfect as it is. We don't normally look at a tree or a dog and say that it is imperfect; yet our discriminating mind tells us we or others are not perfect as we are. Within perfection there is always imperfection and within imperfection there is already perfection. By contrast, since its beginnings Western psychotherapy has been founded on the notion of reaching wellness or wholeness, not necessarily coming from a place where we are already well and whole but from the perspective that we are lacking something.

The other major difference is in the end result that psychotherapy and Zen are aiming for. In Zen we could say the goal is to realize that there is no goal or aim. In psychotherapy the aim is to improve the person's life. Zen is not at all about that.

In psychotherapy there is always hope and fear; in Zen there is neither hope nor fear. Zen and particularly Big Mind will go where psychotherapy won't dare go out of fear of complete dissolution of ego/self. In Zen practice, the dropping off of body/mind is crucial. In current Western psychotherapy there is still a self, even if it is seen as unsubstantial; in Zen, there is no-self, and that no-self is the true self.

I believe that the true Zen experience of no-self, *sunyata*, is outside the realm of the older forms of Western psychotherapy. A real Zen experience of emptiness cannot be conceptual and is hard to attain without years of serious Zen training under a qualified

Zen teacher or master. For the self there is tremendous resistance to losing itself completely, but it is absolutely necessary for a genuine awakening. The introduction of neurobiology, mindfulness and quantum physics into psychotherapy is bringing more and more awareness of change, uncertainty, and the fluid nature of self. But without practice, Big Mind and other skillful means to deeply integrate the client's insight, their realization becomes just another concept.

On the other hand, in Zen there are many shadows that go unnoticed or are disowned. Since in the Zen tradition we place so much value on losing or dropping the self, we easily fall into denial of the existence of a self, even a relative, ever-changing unfixed self. When we look in we see no-self, so what self needs working on? We see that "I am perfect, complete and whole just as I am." We see no need for Western psychotherapy.

This is a huge problem for Buddhist practitioners and communities. We see no-self is perfect as it is, and then we think the self is perfect as it is, which couldn't be further from the truth. Even though from the absolute perspective the self is perfect just as it is, from the relative perspective it can always be further refined and accomplished.

There is a strong tendency in all of us to make what we do and believe in right, and others wrong. We are all conditioned by our upbringing and culture, and cling to old ideas of right and wrong, good or bad. The more we have invested in our way, the more we value it over others'.

The longer we practice either Zen or Western psychotherapy the more we become stuck in our particular point of view. There are those who believe these perspectives are not mutually exclusive, but the ego's need — we all have it! — to be right and make others wrong is deeply ingrained. What will it take to overcome this polarization?

Personally, I am deeply grateful to the many extraordinarily compassionate and skillful men and women professionals in the fields of psychotherapy and psychiatry whom I have encountered and worked with over the years both before and after becoming a student and teacher of Zen. They have helped me profoundly both in my personal life and in my teaching.

I have often written and spoken about how the Big Mind process has its roots in both Zen and the insights of Western psychology. At the same time, as those who have studied with me or followed my work know, I have always said that the Big Mind process is not a form of psychotherapy, and I am a Zen teacher, not a psychotherapist.

I think the divide between Zen and psychotherapy is gradually being bridged in the actual experience of practitioners in both fields. I have seen it happening among Zen teachers and therapists who are my contemporaries and students, including some who are accredited both as Zen teachers and psychiatrists or psychotherapists. And I am increasingly impressed and encouraged by the passionate aspiration I see in practicing therapists and psychiatrists who are being introduced to Big Mind to find a way to bring their experience of the process into their professional work. Just as I have stood on the shoulders of my predecessors in my evolution as a teacher of Zen, I hope they will stand on mine.

I envision a non-dual approach to psychotherapy as a way to both study the self and drop our identification with it, in order to live a healthier and more joyful life. I see it as a foundation for a new psychotherapy embracing both Eastern and Western philosophy and psychology. I believe it is already taking root and evolving through the experience of other practitioners, and nothing would please me more than if it were to continue to do so.

This way of working with the self comes from, and leads to the Apex, embracing and transcending both Dharma and Buddha, Dharma defined as all manifestations of reality and Buddha as awakened or perfection. Using the image of a triangle, one side is Dharma, or all selves, and the other side is Buddha, or no-self or beyond-self. The Apex is an ever-changing, unfixed process that includes and embraces all selves as intrinsically perfect, complete and whole. It goes beyond their individuality or separateness, and is not attached to any particular self, or to non-attachment either.

True psychological health and well-being arise when all these aspects of self, including no-self, function harmoniously together like a company that knows and appreciates all its employees and produces the finest product. The CEO of the company, the final authority, whom I refer to as the Apex or 'me,' takes care of its employees by truly listening to each and every one of them, awakening and empowering each to serve its highest purpose.

This process of empowerment begins with simply asking each one to speak and clarify what its job is. We can ask each voice to speak first as disowned and not yet known or appreciated. Every voice wants to be heard, recognized, loved and appreciated. When it isn't, it acts out in covert and hostile ways that sabotage and undermine the whole system.

When it's held down in the basement unheard, without food or water, not to mention a TV, computer, or smartphone, it will function immaturely, even unhealthily or pathologically. It damages itself and others. Under extreme circumstances it can come out in such negative and harmful ways as addictions and narcissism. These same voices when owned and given an opportunity to speak, to be embodied and empowered, will transcend themselves and function in positive, healthy and mature ways.

When a voice is asked to imagine what it would be like to be owned, honored and appreciated it begins to see its potential to serve the whole system and come to maturity and psychological well-being. The more each disowned voice is awakened, owned, embodied and empowered, the more the whole system realizes its fullest potential and capacity. This allows each aspect or self to move from a negative to a positive functioning, to health and appreciation of all life, its own as well as others'.

The next stage after including and embodying is to detach and gain freedom from each state of mind. Detaching from and not being identified with an aspect of the self is different from disowning, in that it appreciates each voice as pure, perfect, and whole and yet is no longer attached to, or run by any particular voice.

When selves are seen as intrinsically perfect, complete and whole, they are appreciated as awakened and therefore Buddha. The Buddha said that all sentient beings have the same virtue and wisdom as the Buddha. This means that all aspects of mind, or voices, are Dharma and therefore Buddha. There is no Dharma apart from Buddha and no Buddha apart from Dharma. All Buddhas are Dharma and all Dharmas are Buddha. All sentient beings are Buddha and all Buddhas are sentient beings, and every aspect of the whole, since it is a Dharma manifesting as Buddha, is a perfect manifestation of wisdom and compassion, is Buddha-Dharma.

As I like to say, we human beings have two sides, the human and the being, the personal and the impersonal. The human has all the potential to feel, and to be damaged. The being side just is, there is an absence of emotions, fear or damage.

There is a relative as well as an absolute side to this one reality, a fullness as well as an emptiness as complete human beings. To be a well-functioning human being it is necessary to acknowledge, embrace and transcend both sides as the Apex. This is where Zen and Western psychotherapy have the potential to meet.

18

From Drama to Dharma

The Big Mind process has gone through many transformations, as I have, since I first began using it in June of 1999. I've always seen it as a skillful means for fulfilling our true potential as human beings, but at first my focus was on helping students realize the absolute or transcendent perspective, which I now call the right-hand side of the triangle. Throughout history and even in the Zen tradition the transcendent has always eluded us. It was always a hit-or-miss thing, the greater the master the better chance that it was a hit. It requires tremendous awareness and sensitivity on the part of the master, like a hen pecking on the eggshell at precisely the right time, neither too soon nor too late for the chick to emerge.

The Big Mind process, when led by a skilled facilitator, has made a glimpse of the non-dual accessible and predictable for just about anyone open and willing to engage in it. This was what made Big Mind so amazing in the early days, and still does. By just asking to speak to a transcendent voice such as the Awakened Mind, the Buddha, the non-seeking mind, the non-thinking mind, etc., the student has an experience of the Absolute. Thousands of people have experienced this. I believe that the people who doubt that it is possible simply haven't tried or witnessed it.

These days I am much more interested in the Apex or the total triangle. I have named the left side the contracted dualistic self, the right side Big Mind or the non-dual, and the Apex Big Heart, or the Integrating Free-Functioning Human Being, or simply the Aware Self, or Me. Now I am more concerned that people have a Big Heart perspective and live from Big Heart, the Apex, rather than remain in the impersonal non-dual transcendent or Absolute. I see this as true transcendence, which in my thinking includes and yet goes beyond both the relative and the absolute, the personal and the impersonal.

There are many teachers out there who are interested only in transcending the world of suffering and remaining in the non-dual. What I mean by true transcendence is transcending not just the dual but the non-dual as well. When we are in the non-dual we often feel superior to those we see stuck in the dual. There is an absurdity here, because what could be more dualistic than thinking a non-dualistic perspective is superior to a dual?

I am interested in helping people to both ascend and descend the mountain. I have no problem with those who wish to attain to the Absolute or teach from it, but I would also like to work with those who want to come down off the mountain after attaining the summit, to live as truly integrated human beings, not stay apart from the world and the relational aspects of life.

While I was going through the period of intense self-reflection that began in January of 2011, many people wanted me to be farther along in my process than I was. In their eyes a Zen Master should not be grieving or questioning everything as I was. They did not understand why I was suffering like someone who had no realization or understanding.

Some thought I had lost my enlightenment — and that is exactly what happened. I descended the mountain into the world of ordinary human life, suffering like all human beings suffer. This forced me to question all the teachings I had inherited from my Zen tradition, cast away everything that didn't work and strengthen that which did. It has been the greatest opportunity of my life to go beyond what I was taught and discover what is genuine and real for me.

For me these recent years have been like the process of grief associated with loss: denial and loneliness, anger, bargaining, depression, acceptance and finally peace. It is a journey for which there are no shortcuts, nor should there be, even if we wish there were, or if others want to spare us the pain it causes.

Rather than hurrying through it, I saw each step in the process as a koan, with the potential that Zen koans have to teach us when we see them as life, as Dharma. I tried to juice each one completely, as you would an orange in order to make freshly squeezed o.j., before moving on to the next koan or emotion or phase that arose. My practice has been to face the suffering that I caused as well as my own suffering, not to escape it or fall into blame and defensiveness, but to feel and embody it fully and learn from it in every way I can.

I have now spent years looking at where I had gotten stuck or missed the mark, and what I found were some very deeply rooted patterns that blinded me to certain things in my self. I found that some of these patterns go all the way back to my first week of life, some maybe even prior to my birth. Working on them using Big Mind as well as my relaxed way of sitting zazen and the assistance of my mentors and others, I managed to bring clarity and ownership to these patterns, as well as better ways to work on myself and with others, ways I never would have discovered otherwise.

Even though we may understand intellectually how these patterns affect us, it's still difficult to see ourselves clearly, especially to see where we're stuck. People asked me why I didn't see certain places where I was caught. I don't have an answer for them. I have felt for quite some time that rather than asking if we are stuck, the question might be better put, where are we stuck? It may be obvious to others, but that doesn't necessarily mean it is to us. Usually we can't see it until we are no longer stuck there. I couldn't see it then, now I see it all so much more clearly, and I continue to work on my self and my deeply rooted patterns.

I've often said I wouldn't want to do it ever again, but I am so appreciative that I did go through this process and deeply grateful to those who encouraged me to look directly at where I was still stuck. I am what I am today because of these years of self-reflection and practice, and so is Big Mind.

*　　*　　*

What most excites and motivates me these days is exploring how to help people, myself included, enjoy more conscious, deeper, loving relationships, not only with our partner but with others as well. I believe that being mindful of the voice, the perspective, we are coming from, and the patterns that influence our reactions and behavior is crucial to happy and healthy relationships. And the more we are at peace and free within ourselves, the more willing we are to be vulnerable and dwell in our hearts rather than our heads, the easier it is to recognize and deal with the patterns that so powerfully affect our relationships.

I don't believe that we ever get rid of deeply rooted patterns, only that we are able to recognize them and respond appropriately to whatever arises in our life, rather than react in unconscious habitual ways. Our basic insecurity and fear of impermanence give rise to feelings of inadequacy, unworthiness and guilt which lead us to seek validation and approval from others. Without being fully conscious of our own motivations and the patterns from which they arise, we seek power and position. We may feel guilty for not being good enough or worthy of the validation we are seeking. Then instead of being kind and respectful of each other we go round and round, sometimes feeling like a victim without realizing how we are playing that game, sometimes acting as a rescuer, sometimes a perpetrator, sometimes even unaware that we are being unkind or abusive.

This pattern which we keep playing out in our relationships has been aptly called the Drama Triangle. Victim, perpetrator, and rescuer — these are the roles that we seem to unconsciously assume and get stuck in within our relationships, especially the most intimate ones. It is what prevents psychological and emotional equality and transparency and leads to so much suffering in our relationships. We may change roles, but this pattern persists as long as these aspects of ourself remain disowned.

In the Drama Triangle, the victim, when disowned, consciously or unconsciously recruits the perpetrator to perpetrate or the rescuer to rescue, even though their actions often feel like further victimization. Of course this does not mean that there are not real victims and that we cannot be truly powerless in certain situations. It means when we have not yet owned, embodied and empowered our inner victim, we *feel* victimized, even in situations where we are not truly a victim.

The perpetrator when disowned may come out as overbearing and actively aggressive, criticizing, judging and blaming the other in an attempt to prove that we are right. Or it may operate in passive aggressive ways, making the other feel guilty by silently withholding love and energy, in order to get even, thereby keeping the other feeling bad and victimized.

The victim plays out the "Poor Me" scenario, looking for sympathy, recruiting the other to be the perpetrator to confirm the situation, or the rescuer to fix it. When the rescuer comes out in a disowned way it is often led by guilt, or a sense of being responsible for not doing enough. This in turn reinforces the victim's negative feelings, keeping him or her dependent, feeling like a failure or just plain bad.

In the dejected and passive position of the victim, we feel blocked from being empowered, making decisions, solving problems, experiencing pleasure, being happy and self-realized. We feel victimized, oppressed, helpless, hopeless, powerless and ashamed, because we haven't yet owned, embodied, and empowered the one who is truly powerless and vulnerable.

What would it take to transform the Drama Triangle? To begin with we would need to be aware and mindful, owning and taking responsibility for our part in the drama. But this is not so easy, particularly in a close or intimate relationship, even if both parties are doing their best to be aware when they are falling into the drama and are sincerely committed to not getting recruited into one of the three roles.

It is difficult for a couple of reasons: one is deeply rooted patterns from childhood, another is because we all want so desperately to be right and are unwilling to admit our responsibility. So we get stuck in a particular corner of the triangle, or we switch roles, going from victim to rescuer to perpetrator and so on.

Most of us have a deep dislike of being, or being seen as, a victim. Though we may wish to be seen as innocent of any wrongdoing, it is humiliating to own our powerlessness and the victim in ourselves. It is also hard for most of us to recognize, admit and own that we are perpetrating when we are acting out our anger and aggression overtly, even harder when we are doing it covertly.

We often want to help the other, but when we feel powerless to do so our frustration and anger may lead us to act aggressively and abusively. Or we come across as the knower, the authority, or the scolding, judgmental and critical parent. Having become the unacknowledged passive perpetrator in this scenario we often feel wrongly accused, pleading our innocence. "But I'm just trying to help you!" We don't want to see that our very impulse to help and fix the situation can be interpreted by the other as an act of perpetration.

The common thread in these scenarios is that the voices involved in the Drama Triangle are most damaging when they are disowned. This is true of any disowned voice, and it is where the Big Mind process can be tremendously helpful, because it teaches us that owning a voice is not just a matter of intellectual understanding. Understanding, as I like to say, is the booby prize. Owning a voice means becoming one with it, identifying with it completely, embodying it.

When we make that shift, what we discover — most strikingly with voices that we dislike and resist owning — is that the voice when owned is nothing like what we expected, may in fact feel like the opposite of what we thought it would. At the same time, we realize that each voice or unawakened self when owned and awakened has, as the Buddha said of all sentient beings, the same wisdom and compassion as the Buddha.

When we haven't yet owned, embodied, and empowered the one who is truly powerless we see ourself as victimized by others and by life. In our dualistic consciousness we feel vulnerable and separate from other people and from the world. In the Buddha Way this of course is viewed as an illusion, and is referred to as ignorance.

When we own, embody and empower our innate powerlessness, it transforms into power. In Zen this is seen as surrendering to the fact that we are truly powerless and opening ourself up to being empowered by the source, the Dharma, thus becoming a conduit for this great and limitless power.

In other words, when we have not yet realized and actualized our true nature we fall into the patterns described by the Drama Triangle. However, each of us has the capacity to own, embody, and empower these three voices. When our perpetrator is owned and awakened it has the capacity to manifest as our protector. When the victim is fully owned as powerlessness and vulnerability, we can awaken to our true power. And the rescuer fully owned can manifest as a Bodhisattva, no longer about fixing and rescuing from an immature and fearful place, but able to use power appropriately, coming from wisdom and compassion for the sake of awakening all sentient beings as well as oneself.

Integrating these realizations and letting go of old patterns, especially in our most intimate relationships, can't just happen overnight. We all can get caught in the need to be 'right.' Pride plays a tremendous role here. As long as we are stuck in this need to be right, we will never overcome the Drama Triangle.

To let go of our fixed position, step back, and face our fear of being or looking wrong takes a deep commitment to this transformation on both sides. But the alternative, the separation we feel from our loved one, the shutting down that happens when we are caught in this dynamic, is even more painful. All I can say is it takes a lot of hard work, discipline, trust, love and courage to transform the Drama Triangle to the Dharma Triangle.

THE VIEW FROM THE APEX

19

The View from the Apex

When we are faced with the questions life brings up for all of us, the answers from either the relative or the absolute perspective are at best partial. To answer these questions in a way that really makes sense and is helpful in our life, I believe they have to be viewed from the perspective of the Apex, which includes and transcends the other two, the personal, dualistic, relative reality, and the impersonal, non-dual, absolute reality.

To be clear, the self who is speaking in the following pages is coming from the Apex. It is the voice of the Apex, which is innate and accessible in each of us, which resonates in you because it is innate within you. The endless process of integrating its perspective, its wisdom functioning as compassion, into our life is what I call 'practice.'

WHAT IS THE MEANING AND PURPOSE OF THIS LIFE?

To live it fully and completely, not to waste it, but to give it meaning. If we don't give our life meaning it has none. When we live just to satisfy our limited desires and wants we can't seem to find meaning and purpose. If we always put ourself first, then we live a shallow, unproductive and unfulfilling life. When we truly appreciate who we are and what this life is, its meaning and purpose cease to be such a mystery.

The human side of our nature as human beings is full of wants, needs, emotions, feelings, sensations, hurts, pains, and suffering, as well as the ability to love and care for others, to do and to act. The being side is perfect complete and whole just as it is, there is absolutely nothing lacking, nothing in excess and nothing to do — just be.

When we look out at the world, we tend to divide everything into opposites: male and female, high and low, good and bad, right and wrong, young and old, life and death. But each of these opposing pairs are separate only as concepts that we have created. In reality they are one whole.

Life and death are inseparable, two aspects of one reality. From birth comes life, suffering and pleasure and all of that — and death, which is simply a continuation of what we call life. Only what is born dies; that which was never born does not die, and that is our True Self.

To see this we need to take a step back, but that step is not easy. It requires forgetting one's self, or stepping out of the self we are so identified with and attached to. We think we are this one we call the self, but if that's true then who is it that is actually witnessing and observing this self? If we were to look at the one witnessing in this very moment, we would find no one, or no-thing. Who is that? That is what in Zen we sometimes refer to as the 'Forever Unnameable It.' It is not what we think of as the self or the ego; it is the True Self.

The ego self is not the limitless and unconditioned Self, even though we might like it to be and sometimes act as if it were. We believe it is substantial, real and solid. But when we try to find it, it eludes us.

We have a sense that we are not just our name, our story, or what we do, but we don't know who we are. We cover up this not knowing with pretending to know and understand, but in truth we don't know, we're confused and pretend we're not. Or we are caught in our confusion. We fill up our time with trivial pursuits and distractions, all so we don't have to face that we really don't know.

Our problem is that we believe there is something about our situation that needs to be fixed, something we need to know or to do. In fact there is nothing to do. We think we can figure it all out, finally understand and grasp the ungraspable. We can't.

It is beyond our grasp, forever ungraspable and unknowable,

but our ego doesn't like that. The ego always feels it should be able to know what is unknowable and to grasp the ungraspable. That is our human arrogance; monkeys and dogs and all other living beings are not bothered by not knowing, only man is. Dogs are just dogs, monkeys just monkeys, trees are trees.

When we are one with the Absolute or Truth then there is nothing to figure out. When we allow ourself to rest in our True Self, the reality of our nature, then we can relax and be at peace in our Self.

Why aren't we happy just being? Why do we always want to be different or better or greater than we are? We are already perfect. We could spend less time trying to become perfect and more time just being. Our beingness is intrinsically perfect, nothing lacking or extra. From the beginning we are whole, complete and perfect. When we do, just do. When we are not busy doing, then just be.

WHY WE SUFFER

We suffer because we see ourself as separate from our Self. For that matter, we see ourself as separate from everything. We think and act as if we are the center of the universe and everything revolves around us. That is our arrogance again.

We are not separate from everything, in fact we are not separate from anything. What we do affects everyone and everything else, and what everyone and everything does affects us. It is like a giant net, everything is connected to and affects everything else.

We suffer because we are attached to ourself and all that we call "me," "my," and "mine." We cling to them because we think we are separate. We are perfect and whole, and yet we are deluded and confused.

If we would just accept that the Being side of our nature is perfect and whole and yet our human ego side is deluded and confused, everything would be OK, but we don't. So we suffer.

How we delude ourselves

It's actually simple but we make it complicated. When we admit that we are ignorant, then we are wise. When we admit that we are confused, then we are clear. The deluded think they are enlightened, the enlightened know they are deluded. The unwise think they are wise, the wise know they are unwise. The foolish think they are clever, the clever know they are but fools. The insane believe they are sane, the sane realize they are insane. The sinner thinks he is a saint, a saint knows he is but a sinner. It is the foolish who judge everyone else and believe they themselves are perfect. The awakened know that no matter how much they try, the limited and contracted self will never be perfect.

To see how foolish and deluded we are we only need to look at ourselves truthfully. We are so busy trying to be honest with others, yet we are dishonest with ourselves. We judge others and are rude and selfish, yet we think of ourselves as good and righteous. Our face is a mask. We are afraid to reveal ourselves to others and, more importantly, to ourselves.

We won't admit and own the fact that we are self-centered and arrogant, that we lie, steal, judge, condemn, and hate. That we are fools acting as if we are wise and good. We are unique, perfect and complete and yet we believe that we are unworthy, insufficient and inadequate.

Take stealing for example: we are constantly stealing — attention, time, love, as well as others' ideas and property. We steal their integrity and their good name with our gossip. We condemn and speak ill of others' faults as if we ourselves were pure and perfect. We put others down in order to elevate ourselves and inflate our own ego. We act proper and pious in front of others; when we are alone and no one can see us we are more honest, we pick our nose, we fart. If we place such value on honesty and integrity, shouldn't we first admit, at least to ourselves, that we are self-centered, and hypocritical?

We may be able to hide from others, but we can't hide from ourselves. Being mindful and attentive means not hiding from ourselves, but seeing who and what we really are. It doesn't take years of meditation to do that. We have the potential to be happy, but we fight our own happiness by trying so hard to be right and look good to others. Then we ask why we suffer.

WHAT TO DO ABOUT CONFUSION

Confusion is only a problem because we dislike it. If we didn't, it wouldn't be a problem. Like so many aspects of ourself that we reject and consider wrong or bad, confusion can be our ticket to liberation and freedom from suffering. We needn't try to get rid of confusion or seek after clarity. It is our preference for clarity over confusion that keeps us bound up without even a rope. In fact it is our attachment to all of our preferences that makes life so difficult for us. We can even have a preference for no preference — that's how insane we can be.

If we speak to confusion and ask what it wants from us, if we treat it with respect and appreciate it as we would one of our own children, then confusion will function for us in a profound way we would never have expected. Confusion might answer something like this: 'I know I am unwelcome, and that makes me feel bad and wrong. I have a lot to offer and yet I don't feel appreciated and recognized. What I would like is to be honored, loved and empowered.'

When we fear that confusion already has so much power over us, it takes courage to ask what it could offer us if we were to acknowledge and empower it. But what do we really have to lose? We may discover that confusion when empowered actually transforms into clarity.

When we no longer resist confusion we can completely relax and be ourself. Our True Self, not our pretend or adopted self, always trying to appear as if we know and understand everything. We can be free from worrying about looking foolish or worse, stupid. Just imagine how liberating it would be to simply admit that I am stupid and deluded.

Making friends with fear

We fear fear because we don't understand its purpose. When we honor and appreciate it we understand that fear is actually alertness and awareness, a mind that is awake and attentive to all. When fear is suppressed it comes out in the way that we know it, immature and unhealthy.

We fear it because we have never owned and embraced it, except perhaps in our athletic and daredevil pursuits. If we would embrace it in our pursuit of happiness, wisdom and well-being, we would discover how to befriend it and be free. When fear is disowned, it holds us down and turns into anxiety and illness. It keeps us trapped and stressed, especially when it prompts us to suppress other emotions like anger and resentment, which many of us were taught are wrong and bad. We fear anger because we do not trust ourself or have faith that we can handle our anger. We hang on to control, afraid to let go, and so we fight against our true nature and resist being free to be ourself. Fear keeps us small and contracted, limited by our lack of faith which finally is our only true ailment.

We need to make friends with our fear. It is there to protect us from doing stupid and careless things, to be aware of potential dangers and people who don't have our best interest at heart. We need to empower fear as a warrior, an awakened mind, open and alert, ready to spring into action when necessary, otherwise just poised and aware. When we empower fear to do its job, it becomes an ally, a great friend that is always conscious and aware, a true guardian and protector.

Disappointment

Like fear, disappointment is a great ally in disguise. It allows us to lose our illusions and our naivety. It is an inevitable and important, though painful part of the process of growing up and maturing.

We rarely deal with disappointment in a mature and healthy

way. Very often we blame the one who breaks our heart or disappoints us rather than taking responsibility for our projections. It is hard to accept responsibility for our part of the process, to acknowledge that we are not so innocent, and appreciate its lessons. We tend to blame, to become the victim, rather than own and acknowledge our role. This is why there is so much guilt, aggression and trying to fix and change others, instead of loving and appreciating them for who and what they are.

LONELINESS AND THE ILLUSION OF SEPARATENESS

Instead of trying to escape from loneliness as we normally do, if we face it and sit with it, we will find that loneliness flips into 'I alone am,' very different from loneliness. Loneliness is based in the delusion that we are separate from everyone and everything else, which is just not so. It merely reflects our deeply held view that we are the center of the universe and everything and everyone revolves around us and is separate from us.

When we expand our awareness to a wider perspective, we realize that our consciousness has no limits, that our mind and heart are boundless and infinite. Then there is no other, there is no discrete, lonesome me. We are one with all things and all things are one me. When we drop the illusion of separateness we see that from the beginning all things are but manifestations of Dharma and are not separate from us. They never were; it was just an illusion. From this perspective we are no longer lonely but all one (alone).

The illusion of separateness comes from our mind. Our ability to think and to make distinctions is a great gift, and it is absolutely necessary for our survival to be able to distinguish between oneself and everything else. However this gift comes with a cost: fear. Because we have the ability to see things as separate, we are aware of danger, which reinforces the illusion of self and other.

But understanding this conceptually does not relieve our loneliness. What we need is a true realization of it, where all doubt is eliminated, a deep awakening in which this subject-object division disappears, where we truly get without a shadow of a doubt, "it's all ME!" There is no other; the delusion that others exist separate from me, is the illusion that creates our dissatisfaction and suffering.

We are only lonely again if we fall back into the concept of a separate self. We can choose to do this as a very advanced practice, after we have been aligned for a long time with our limitless Self, in order to know what it is like to feel the pain others feel. When we have spent too long on top of the mountain we forget the suffering of our fellow human beings, their feelings of loneliness, of inadequacy and unworthiness. Then it is time to come down off the mountain. Only then can we truly help others, not by preaching or even by trying to reach down to them from above, but by being completely with them in their suffering and loneliness.

OWNING OUR OPPOSITES

Whatever aspect of ourselves we own and embody, its opposite must also be owned and embodied. However we see ourself, we are at the same time, the opposite of what we see. If we think we are deluded, then we need to see that we are also enlightened. If we see ourself as stupid, then we also have genius within. If we finally realize that we are Zen, then we must eventually drop this realization and see we are equally not Zen. Spiritual, then we are not spiritual too. A good person, then we are also an asshole.

The opposite is always present and if it is not acknowledged it will act out covertly. By owning and empowering the opposite we free ourselves from whatever we are identified with.

GETTING A HANDLE ON OUR ADDICTIONS

In my view we have but one addiction and that is to our self and everything we label me, my or mine. This is our fundamental addiction, all the others follow from it. We see ourself as separate from everyone and everything else, and this leads us down the slippery slope of attachment to drugs, alcohol, sex, money, power, food, fame and success.

The problem with seeing everything as separate and outside ourself is that we lose our power and seek it in all the wrong places. We believe either that we have no control over our addictions or that we can control them — and then we continue to fail over and over again. The key to facing our addictions is acknowledging that we are addicted and accepting that we are powerless. However that is only half the real solution. To take back our power we need to own that our contracted self is not separate from our limitless Self which is one with all things.

Our limitless Self, the Forever Unnamable, what we may call God, is within and not separate from who we truly are. We ask God, Why am I powerless and feeling helpless in my life, particularly in the face of my addictions? It is because we give our power away instead of claiming it as our birthright.

We feel small and inadequate when we put God or the Unnamable outside ourself. Of course we are rightly wary of owning God or Buddha within us. That very thought sounds like the textbook definition of delusion, if not insanity. Infinite potentiality manifests as us and through us, but it would be arrogant to think our self, the ego, is that Source. However, unless we see that Buddha is within each of us and that each of us is Buddha, we give our power away. By owning that Buddha is not separate from us, we can re-own the power that will enable us to deal with our addictions.

SURRENDERING TO POWERLESSNESS

In the spiritual world seeking truth or awakening is OK, but seeking power is considered in bad taste or much worse. When we feel inadequate and powerless we don't like to admit that we really do want power. However, the truth is that the limited, small, contracted self is ultimately powerless. We are born powerless, we grow old, become ill and weak, and eventually die powerless. Whatever power we gain through position, wealth, insight or title doesn't alter the fact that we are powerless to begin with, and in the end. We only have the power that others give us. Ultimately we are powerless and by acknowledging and owning this fact we find our real power.

Everything in life is forcing us to acknowledge this reality. Our life is impermanent, vulnerable and fragile. It is why we feel like victims or use what power we have in immature and unhealthy ways, or inflate ourselves by trying to rescue or save others. We even try to use powerlessness as a weapon, a means to acquire power, to feel more powerful or empowered. It is all about escaping from the fact that we are powerless.

The point is to give up trying to escape it, to surrender and acknowledge that we are powerless and any power we might have is an illusion, here today gone tomorrow. It is said that the truth will set us free, and that truth is power. To put it more precisely, awakened to the truth we are empowered by truth, set free by the truth. The truth is there was never anything to gain, and no escape.

We are born powerless and will die powerless and everything in between is delusion. When we surrender to this fact we are set free to live life with honesty, dignity and humility. When we truly come to terms with our powerlessness we live a life that is happy, free and giving.

OUR PROBLEM IS THAT WE LACK REAL TRUST

Our problem is that we lack real trust, trust that would turn our life around 180 degrees. From this lack of trust or faith, fear and doubt arise. Not that fear and doubt are bad, only that they too are in the basement and cannot function properly to serve us. What would happen if we were to accept our delusion and realize that all our effort to be free from delusion is causing us unnecessary suffering?

We always want to be where and what we are not. We don't know how to be satisfied with what we are. We want to be different, better, greater. We are lacking absolutely nothing, but we still believe otherwise. That is our delusion. To realize nothing is lacking, that intrinsically we are already perfect, complete and whole is to be awakened, free and at peace.

The moment we realize who we are, we realize that there was never any enlightenment to seek after, that our only delusion was thinking something was missing. It is as if we thought we had lost our head and ran around looking for it as Enyadatta did, which would be completely deluded, and frankly quite stupid. If we then got all excited about finding it, that would also be quite stupid, even bordering on insane. Since we were never missing our head in the first place, to think we are special and great after we find it is ridiculous, and a further delusion.

Relaxing and realizing it was never lost, and that finding it was no big deal, is what is call "beyond enlightenment." We can then go on and live our life in a natural and ordinary way, just being who and what we are.

FAITH

What I mean by trust may become clearer if we call it by another name: faith. Faith is not to be confused with belief, which is in something outside ourself, whereas true faith is in our limitless True Self. Faith is pure, belief is tricky. Belief in anything outside ourself is not faith but an expectation — or a hope, which we also get wrong.

Hope, like belief, causes us to give our power away. This can work for us up to a point, but always ends in disappointment. We feel forsaken or worse, betrayed. God or Buddha doesn't let us down; we do that to ourselves, by separating from God and then believing it is all God's responsibility, blaming rather than taking responsibility for ourself and our actions. When we do take full responsibility for our disappointment, recognizing that it was based on belief, expectations, hope and false faith, then we discover true faith.

When faith and belief in some thing outside our self are dropped, true faith is always there. It is the bottom line, we can't lose it. Faith, not in something, not in a limited self, not in another, but in no 'thing.' It was there from the beginning, it it is always with us. That, and possibly our past life karma, is all we are born with.

Unconditional faith may come more easily to some than to others. We all have the potential for it, in fact it is our birthright. However, depending on our level of fear and how cut off we are from our True Self, true faith is a struggle. When we can let go of our preconceived ideas of who we are and what we believe we know, then faith appears. Real faith is always there, but manifests only when our opinions, beliefs and concepts are dropped. When we reach the place of true not-knowing then we find the faith that was always present within us, our very ground of being. Faith is in no-thingness and this is our limitless or True Self, not our contracted, limited self.

THE ONENESS OF LIFE

Most of us have not worked through our fear of loss, especially loss of self and who we believe we are. We cling to our identity for dear life, because we think our identity *is* our life instead of a persona we take on, a role we play in order to be known and seen by the world. Beginning in childhood, we created this identity out of necessity, to survive. Not that there is anything wrong with our particular identity; it's just something we created which is not our True Self. Our True Self is what is there when we drop that persona. It is what is beneath what we think of as our identity.

When we go through fear and discover our true identity we gain wisdom, the wisdom of realizing who we really are, which is our True Self, our True Nature. Our wisdom is that we are one with and not separate from all things. That we are boundless and infinite and yet finite and limited. That we are all things and yet completely unique and special. That we create this life and yet experience the limitations of our karma. That we create our karma from moment to moment and yet cannot escape it. That we are never free from cause and effect and our only choice is to be one with our karma. That when we resist cause and effect we suffer. That none of us is an island unto ourself, but connected and interdependent with all things.

We see just how simple and uncomplicated life is. We see all as equal and realize compassion for all. We cease being so judgmental and opinionated. We realize the oneness of life and that we are no better or worse than anyone else. In fact what we realize is that we are all one body/mind. We then function more selflessly with more generosity and forgiveness.

THE POWER OF DOUBT

Doubt is the other side of faith. True faith is comfortable with doubt and can doubt everything, including our faith. It could even be said that to doubt is not only healthy, but absolutely necessary in order to uncover true faith, which is unconditional and has been there from the beginning.

If we really wish to know truth we must go through doubt, which means questioning everything — all we think we know and believe and all we have been taught to believe to be true. We must question all our concepts, beliefs, ideas, opinions and especially ourself. There is nothing too sacred to be questioned and doubted completely. No stone should be left unturned, no certainty unquestioned. Doubt is no other than the seed of true awakening to realizing who we are: Buddha.

We need to realize there is absolutely nothing to rely on, nothing to be grasped or attained. Truth is not a 'thing' that can be attained; it is all there is and is not. That there is nothing which can be attained *is* the Truth. All those who have truly known this have confirmed that it is the absolute truth. When we realize without any doubt that we have attained absolutely nothing, how can it be doubted or questioned, since there is no claim or thought of having realized or attained anything? This is the true liberation and peace of mind that we are searching for so desperately.

GOD

God is each one of us for God is no other than our limitless and True Self and is, in fact, all things as well as no things. Wherever we look we see only God. God's shape and color is everywhere.

It is like the wind when it blows through the trees and grasses, through the blue sky and white clouds. The color of the mountains and rivers. The beautiful smile on a child's innocent face and the horrible cries of agony after a bomb has exploded in a crowd. God can be seen in all and yet we don't see God. God looks like me, you and our neighbors, and the faces of those from other nations and races.

The Source or God has always been from beginningless time and will always be throughout endless time. It has no form and is all forms. It is colorless and yet all colors. It has no shape and yet is all shapes and sizes. God is odorless and yet all smells are God.

We cannot see God, yet wherever we look there It is. It is nowhere, yet everywhere. All sounds are the sound of God, yet God is not a sound, It is soundless. It is not anything and yet It is all things and in all things and yet no thing.

Look for God and you cannot find It, but God is right here always. Our mind cannot grasp the forever ungraspable, yet let go and we cannot lose It. Search everywhere and we cannot find God, yet who is it that is searching?

In my view there is but one God, and yet God is numberless. It is within each one of us and everyone and all things as innumerable as all the sands of all the oceans in the world. It is known by many names, but is forever nameless, the Forever Unnameable It.

All names limit God for then It becomes a man-made concept. No concept can reach God and what and who It is, and yet all concepts are also God. It can't and won't be limited by man, and yet It is every word and thought. Nothing can reach God, yet It is always present.

SPEAKING OF GOD

What we call our self and what we call God are not separate, and yet not one either, both are concepts. God and I are beyond all concepts of God and I. We need to know that we must let go of all notions of the existence of a fixed and solid self within, a fixed and solid self within others, or a universal self. Otherwise our mind will still grasp after such relative concepts. We should also let go of all notions of the non-existence of such concepts.

Everything that I am now saying is also a concept, so when we use such concepts we need to remember they are unreal. We use them much as we would use a boat to cross a river. Once the river has been crossed, the boat is of no further use and should be cast away. So too concepts and ideas, including the concept of non-existence.

If you try to grasp what I am saying with your conceptual mind, you just can't, it's impossible. Let go of trying to grasp it and just allow it in. There is a non-conceptual part of your mind that already understands all I am sharing with you. Just allow these words to be heard by that deeper part within you. It is a profound place that is already fully awakened and has all the wisdom of the ages. It existed before your parents were born and will be present long after your descendants have perished.

FEELING THE PRESENCE OF
THE FOREVER UNNAMEABLE

When we think of the divine, the Forever Unnameable as outside ourself, we not only create an obstacle to true faith, we also have difficulty accepting our own humanity.

Because we haven't known that the Unnameable has always been right here as us, we project It outward, onto an entity outside ourself, sometimes onto our biological parents, teachers, or other important role models in our life. Then, to gain their recognition and unconditional love, we try to live up to some standard they represent for us, and no matter what we accomplish and how hard we work to achieve it, we are likely to remain unsatisfied. Not that our goals are unworthy, but our efforts are exhausting and unfulfilling because in our own eyes and theirs we always fall short.

If we owned and embodied the divine within us we would feel the unconditional love and acceptance we have always longed for. We have nothing to prove. When we fall or fail, this unconditional love is still absolutely present with total forgiveness.

People who feel presence of the Divine in this way sometimes speak of Him as their true personal Father, not their biological father who is another human being with all our human failings and shortcomings. It is a beautiful intimacy and a personal relationship with the Divine that most of us rarely experience, a tender love for us that is sweet and protective, and yet tough too. As long as we separate from it we long to know and be one with God.

IF GOD HAD A VOICE

If God had a voice, and we could hear it, it might sound something like this: 'You are all my children whom I love tenderly and unconditionally. I am so proud of you for just being yourself, for who you are. You don't have do anything to earn my love. You don't need to prove yourself to me as you felt you had to do for your parents and others. I do not need to live vicariously through you as they may have needed to do, for they were only human.

'I am no other than you and therefore I have only unconditional love, acceptance and trust in you. When you look inside you cannot find Me because I am not some thing but rather no-thing, all-pervading and omnipresent. I am always here watching over you. You can relax and put your trust in Me. I will always be here without fail.

'You can see now that your own parents were doing their best and maybe now you can forgive them for their shortcomings and for not always being there to protect you. Now that you know Me intimately, you can free your parents, teachers and other role models from your projections, and love and appreciate them unconditionally for who they were, and are.

'It is not that you don't need to do your best in this life, to live with integrity and love your neighbor. However, you don't need to feel you have to be special and perfect to be loved and accepted by Me; you already are. I love and accept you unconditionally, and still your life is about living up to your true potential and your given nature. You may have thought that somehow you were inherently sinful, but in my eyes you are already perfect, complete and whole. Knowing this, continue to refine and fulfill yourself as a human being.

'It is your thinking that separates you from Me. You can't get to Me in the same way you get other things you are used to achieving. I am beyond all that. I am your ungraspable, ever-present true nature. I am not something you can get to or grasp. However you can experience Me and be one with Me by no longer identifying with the apparent reality of separateness, by leaping in a moment outside of time, from where you are standing to Me, what you would call another reality, My reality. The moment you let go of yourself and all you cling to as you and yours, then you are Me.

'Once you have seen this, in your vanity you may think you *are* Me and your immature and egocentric ego may try to appropriate Me as your own. I can't be possessed by your tiny ego. I am infinite, timeless and boundless. You are finite, within time and bounded; I have nothing to do with time and space. The being side of your nature is Me, and when you drop all, then here I am, your true nature, forever ungraspable by your small, contracted mind.

'Though you cannot grasp Me, you can let go, or even better let be, and I am here, present and accessible. I am where there is no you present, where you are no longer confined by your thinking. You need to get out of your limited and small mind. Going 'out of your mind' may sound frightening to you, because you confuse it with going insane. Actually the way you normally are is insane, and true sanity can only be found in what you project as insanity or madness.

'It is your fear that prevents you from finding Me. You are creating this artificial barrier between us. From the beginning there never was a barrier other than the false one you create. I have always been, from before the Big Bang, and all is available to you as you grow and evolve and learn to rest in non-thinking, in My eternal presence.'

PRAYER

In my experience, prayer works. We don't need to understand how. Do we understand how a fax machine or our cell phones work in order to use them? Why do we think we need to know how prayer works?

One form of prayer is asking a power greater than our limited self for assistance, either for another or others, or for ourself. We pray from an open and humble heart that can receive, placing our palms together, joining our divine nature and our contracted self. What matters is not our form and posture but the sincerity of our attitude. Intentions and thoughts count as well as speech and actions.

The second form of prayer is more contemplative. Rather than always asking for help, we pray from an open-hearted place, just being silent, resting in pure being, doing nothing, asking for nothing, wanting nothing, having nothing, knowing nothing, being nothing. It's not asking for something; it's more like sitting beside a stream and just watching your thoughts pass by without commenting or judging them. Have no preference or judgement for or against anything that arises, and if you do have a preference or judgement, don't judge that.

God is our True Self, is within all and is all, always present to us and yet can't be found or grasped as an object. When we are completely silent and unmoving, just being, we and the Forever Unnameable are most intimate, at One. This is true atonement, at-one-ment. It is here that we may ask for forgiveness. When we are truly coming from here, God will not refuse us.

LOVE, CONDITIONAL AND UNCONDITIONAL

Another name for God is love. Not the emotion we generally think of as love, but the unconditional love which is all there is when the self is dropped and oneness with all things arises. It is what propagates and allows all creatures to survive. It is the most natural way, the love that parents of all species have for their offspring. It brings people together, it binds them to one another. It is the absence of the illusion of separateness. It is pure energy, it is the very ground of being.

Of course the limited and contracted self cannot love unconditionally. When the self is not present, unconditional love is natural and easy; when the contracted self is present, it is not possible. We will always have conditions. That is human nature, and it's OK.

However, not being able to love another unconditionally causes pain and suffering, since any conditions, any hopes of someone fully living up to our expectations will be disappointed. The more we are attached to their being what we want them to be, the more unhappy or dissatisfied we are with their being who and what they are.

Whenever we dislike what is, whether it be a loved one or the conditions we find ourself in, we will suffer. Likewise, we all suffer to some degree when someone we love judges or criticizes us. In short, when we live in the world and choose to be in relationship, we will suffer. But suffering is not all bad. We grow and expand through relationships and even from the suffering we encounter in them.

When we first enter into a relationship, some of the good feelings we call love come from the positive projections we cast on the one we love, and receive from them. When these positive projections get turned for some reason, usually disappointment, it is a very difficult moment in the relationship, and it can last a long time. Some relationships don't survive it.

When this happens communication is essential and right understanding is crucial. We both are responsible for communicating our needs and wishes as well as our disappointments. It is important that we realize it is our own projections on the other that cause our suffering, not the other. We had hoped and wished they would live up to our expectations and projections, but for better or worse they are just being who they are. If we understand that, we can actually come together and grow as human beings.

Most of us do not want to hear this, but it is the way it is. If we expect things or people to be other than the way they are, we will suffer. However we can learn and grow from our suffering and become better, more decent human beings. In every intimate relationship we eventually go through a bonding process, becoming connected and interdependent. Then at some point each one in the relationship will need to reestablish their own independence, which can be surprisingly healthy for both parties. If our attitude is positive and we are doing our best to expand and grow up from our pain and suffering, we will, and it all becomes a teaching for us.

We are in an evolutionary process both as individuals and as a species. It is for us to constantly evolve towards our True Nature which is perfect, complete and whole. We'll never get all the way there as long as we are in a body, but we need not worry about making it to complete perfection. Only the side of us that is divine is perfect — our being side, not our human side. Our human, or doing side will always have more to do. Our being has already arrived, it never left.

We are already perfect and complete just as we are, and we will always be imperfect and incomplete at the same time. In our imperfections we are perfect, and in our perfections we are imperfect. Realizing this, we continue to refine our imperfections and our life.

TRUE EQUALITY

Not only are all people created equal, all beings are created equal as well, and some day we all will see and understand that to be the truth. When we really look an animal in the eyes we see the Divine there, the same as we do when we look into the eyes of another human being.

Some day we humans will realize that all are God's children, not just a few, or one species. We are evolving, however slowly. The more we open our hearts and minds, the more we realize this truth.

WE ALREADY HAVE WHAT WE THINK WE LACK

There is a true treasure within each of us and yet we look for it elsewhere. We seek wisdom and knowledge from others, or from records of their sayings, which we call the Good Book, the Sutras, or the Teachings, as if they contained the Truth. But the Truth we seek is beyond words and letters. We already have everything we seek, it's been within us from birth.

Our humanness and beingness are two of the three treasures we are born with. Our beingness is without beginning or end, it is birthless and deathless, unborn and undying, and neither comes nor goes. It has neither too little nor too much of anything, is without boundaries or limits, eternal and timeless, and cannot be hurt or destroyed. Our humanness enables us to feel, to cry, to be happy or sad. We have the capacity to love and hurt, to be kind to one another or to be cruel.

We can be attached and suffer, or detach from our notion of self and be liberated. Our capacity to attach, even to not being attached, is endless, and our ability to do harm is also endless. These two treasures, our humanness and our beingness, are inseparable, they cannot be divided. Together they make up our third treasure.

We already have everything we need to be free, and joyful, and most importantly to appreciate this life we are blessed with, to be kind, loving, and considerate and act with wisdom and compassion towards ourself and others. We ask ourself how we should live. Why don't we begin by just being a little kinder and more loving to others, to our neighbors, friends and family?

RESTING IN NON-THINKING

Most of us know only the world of thinking. We believe that thinking, and what we can think, is the only reality — that in fact it *is* reality. But that isn't true. Which is why it is so important for us to begin to question everything we believe. There is another reality, an Absolute Reality which lies hidden from us and holds a treasure more precious than all the gold in the world. It is immediately accessible to us, but not to our thinking mind.

We need to learn to rest in non-thinking. This is not to say we need to stop thinking. That would be like telling a child to stop fidgeting. The more we say so, the more he fidgets. Being told to stop thinking only causes us to think more. We need to learn the art of non-thinking, sitting down comfortably and allowing our thinking mind to do what it naturally wants and is meant to do, which is to think. When we give the thinking mind permission to think freely, it gently quiets down on its own.

We may be afraid that if we allow our mind to think freely, it will think bad, even evil thoughts, thoughts that God might punish us for having. We waste so much energy trying to control our minds and avoid thinking what we call bad thoughts, but in God's eyes there is no such thing as a bad thought, they are all just thoughts, empty like bubbles on the surface of the water.

We are the ones who label or divide them into good and bad, right and wrong. As the great Master Dogen says, "Set aside all involvements and let the myriad things rest. Zazen is not thinking of good, not thinking of bad. It is not conscious endeavor. It is not introspection. Do not desire to become a Buddha; let sitting or lying down drop away."

When we stop trying to control our thoughts and instead rest in non-thinking we can begin to loosen our grip on our notions and beliefs, and their hold on us. We have locked ourself in our own prison. We look to others for release — gurus, saints, priests and masters — not realizing that we hold the key to our own liberation, to peace and true happiness. The key is not outside ourself but when we look within we cannot find it either, for it is not a 'thing.'

It is the divine aspect of each of us.

We make it hard to understand when it is actually simple. We complicate it with our limited mind. We cannot get to it by thinking and conceptual thought. We must rest in being and realize what is always present, simply stop doing and just be. It is always here right here now, but only when we stop thinking and grasping for it can we actually find it. The self must disappear, and then it is present and knowable in the midst of not-knowing.

Non-thinking is beyond thinking and not thinking, knowing and not knowing. Knowing, thinking that we know, is our delusion. We know only a fraction of what is.

Imagine that all you know and have ever experienced is sitting exactly where you are sitting at this moment, and that all you don't know and have never experienced is just beyond the self encapsulated in this bag of skin. Now shift and be that, that which is not this limited self, be all that you don't know and have never experienced, beyond time and space, from the beginningless beginning to the endless end. From here look at the self that is attached to and identified with what it knows and its limited experiences.

We think not-knowing is stupidity, but true not-knowing is reality where the separation of subject and object ceases to exist. This is where the self drops off and there is "I alone am." The limitless Self and the contracted self dwell in a profound intimacy beyond knowing and not knowing, beyond thinking and not thinking, beyond seeking and not seeking.

When we seek our True Self we just go further astray because the seeking mind is limited to seeking, not finding. We seek the Way but the seeking mind is not the Way, and yet it is. Our very life is the Way. I am the Way, but this I is not the contracted self, and yet it is. When we try to grasp the limitless Self It is ungraspable. When we close our fist and try to clutch it, it disappears; when we open our hand it is right here.

SITTING

Sit still and just be quiet, listen, like the empty sky allowing every cloud to drift by without hindrance, neither clinging to nor rejecting what enters, not partial to one cloud or another, without preference for or against anything that appears.

This is how to be intimate with our True Nature. This is true meditation, not an exercise to be laboriously practiced. In this profound silence we can hear and understand the silent voice of the Forever Unnameable. But don't try to find it, for if you do you will fail.

Trying to sit is already not sitting. Just as trying to throw a ball is not the same as throwing it, trying to sit is not just sitting. Simply sit and do nothing, seek nothing, expect nothing, have nothing, want nothing.

When and how much you sit is up to you. Sit like this until you are always just being, as you are when you are just sitting, with faith to enter every situation free of preconceived notions or ideas of what will be or what you will say or do. When you are no longer identified only with your thinking mind, there is a balance or harmony of thinking and not thinking, what we can call non-thinking, beyond thinking and not thinking.

This is our true state of being, our most natural state of mind. It is fully awake and open, restful and aware, flexible and unhurried. It is not stuck in any place or perspective. It is free and unmovable, clear and transparent. This is where we are one with all creations and the creator. This is our original mind and true nature. We can't attain to it; we already are it.

WE HAVE CHOICE AND YET WE HAVE NONE

Very little of our life is actually in our control, yet we do have a say in our own destiny. We are creating our future every moment in the present by what we think, say and do. What happens is neither predetermined nor chosen out of what we call free will. Those are merely concepts we have created in our small and limited minds. We have choice and yet we have none.

We do have choice, and with that choice we can choose what is. As long as we want our life to be other than it is, wanting what we already have may sound like stoicism, passivity, giving up. However, if we embraced and appreciated our life moment by moment with the same energy that we often try to change and escape it, we could realize just how precious this life is.

What is important is to awaken moment by moment and not waste this lifetime which we have been given. In all that comes our way the greatest challenges and hardships are opportunities for us to grow and expand. Instead of fearing them, we can see them as a teaching for us to continuously deepen and refine ourself to be more loving and compassionate, happy and free.

We need to realize that our expectations cause us disappointment and unhappiness. To have fewer expectations, to choose what we have and to be where we are, is to intimately know freedom and happiness. There are no accidents, all is cause and effect.

Our position in any given moment in time, where we are and to what degree an action or even non-action is appropriate, creates what is right or wrong in that moment. What is seen as a good thing one moment may be seen as a bad thing the next.

Karma is neither good nor bad; it is how we interpret it that makes it good or bad. Whatever our karma is, rather than resisting it, be one with it; fighting it is not only futile but the cause of great suffering.

CONTEMPLATING DEATH

When we avoid facing that this life as we know it will come to an end we rob ourself of one of life's greatest treasures. By contemplating death and realizing our mortality we learn to more fully appreciate life, our own life and all things, even inanimate objects, the rivers, mountains, seas, and valleys and all the creatures on this beautiful planet, the tiniest things, the smallest opportunities to be with loved ones and people who love us.

When we realize that our life will come to an end we have awakened to the truth of impermanence. All things that are born or come into existence are impermanent and will die or cease to exist in the form and the way they do. We may try to ignore or deny it, as if life were permanent, but of course no one and no thing can escape it.

This is the wisdom of no escape. When we realize it, we are ready to look at our life from an entirely fresh perspective. This is awakening the mind and heart of wisdom, seeing that life is swiftly passing by, and that the opportunity to grow, develop and be aware are easily lost or squandered. We begin to treat every moment as an occasion to further awaken to our capacity as human beings to be happy and joyous for no apparent reason.

HEAVEN AND HELL

Why worry about what will happen to us after death? We will find out then. What difference does it make to know that now? We are just projecting our fears into the future. Past and future are just concepts in our mind — making us either regret our past or fear our future. More important is how we are living in this life, here and now.

We worry about a heaven when it is within our reach right here now. We fear what we imagine could happen in an imaginary future. But the future doesn't exist, and neither does the past. There is only NOW, there is only HERE, there is only ME. Heaven and hell exist right here, we are creating them, every moment.

When we are attached to things, to self and others, we create the possibility of loss. When we lose what we cherish, we are in hell. When we do not get attached to self or to others, human or non-human, we create heaven.

However, to live without being attached to loved ones and others is the way of the coward. May as well die. When we consciously choose to live with attachments we are choosing to suffer, to enter hell. But we can learn to enjoy our visit and experience life in hell fully and completely. When we do this, hell is heaven; when we stay detached and removed from life, heaven is hell.

What we need to learn is how to be kinder, more honest, transparent, and loving, more understanding of our fellow beings. We can make the decision to be happy and joyful, to stop blaming others, even God, for everything that we don't like, and take responsibility for our own actions, and reactions.

We have within us both the worst of the worst and the best of the best. It is only because we haven't been driven to do certain terrible things that we feel superior to others. We need to cease denying our confusion, ignorance, greed, anger and fear, to stop pretending that we know who we are, and own the fact that we don't know.

When we see and realize that we are all connected and dependent on one another, that no one is an island unto him- or herself, that all are created equal in our true nature, then it makes perfect sense to treat others as we ourselves want to be treated, to be more compassionate and empathetic towards all beings including our Mother Earth.

CROSSING TO THE OTHER SHORE

The journey from where we are in our life, with our difficulties and sorrows, losses and disappointments, to a place where we will be happy, satisfied, free and at peace is described in Buddhist and other traditions as crossing to the other shore. For this journey it seems we need a raft constructed of the proper materials: meditation, chanting, bowing, mindfulness, attentiveness, surrender, submission, Sutras, Buddhist and other teachings, gurus, teachers, masters and other skillful means.

Now, there is a slow way to make this journey, and a fast way. The sudden and immediate way is to realize we are already on the other shore. There were never two shores, only one — which turns out to be here right now. Thinking there was ever anything to cross over or go through was an illusion. We have been desperately trying to get home, only to realize that we are already there, and there was never any place to go. We were always home, here, it was crazy to think we weren't. Where else could we be?

The slow way can take years of raft-building and rowing. It takes time, often lots of time, to completely cross over to the other shore. Meanwhile we become strongly attached the raft, since it is constructed from all the ideas and practices taught us by those who believe they are necessary to cross over, teachers who put their trust in the raft, not in the realization that there has never been anywhere to go. They don't see that there never were two shores.

The journey to the other shore or the other side was always an illusion. It was a gateless gate to begin with, there was no gate and nothing to pass through. There was no goal to be attained, nothing to gain.

Some teachers and masters do say this; some don't. The great ones say it over and over again, but either people don't believe them or can't hear them, or can't let go of the raft. Finally all the teachings and practices were part of the raft to be discarded.

There is just this life to live freely as oneself and it was never necessary to become something or someone else. We are originally whole, complete and perfect. We were created this way, as all creations without exception are. Only our lack of faith and our attachment to our mistaken views keep us from realizing it.

AN EXTRAORDINARY TIME IN HUMAN HISTORY

This is an extraordinary time in human history. More and more of us are coming closer to enlightenment and beginning to wake up to our true presence within. I don't believe there has ever been such a time before. We are coming out of a very dark period and evolving as a species. Our journey is endless and eternal.

Remember life is life and death is death. Life does not become death, just as the mulch from a tree does not become a tree again but gives life to many trees. A tree has its life and purpose; mulch has its life and purpose. They are not the same and yet not different either.

We have the great good fortune to witness our evolution as human beings. All that is asked of us is to wake up to what we are doing, thinking and saying, for it all matters, it all has consequences. And remember, within our happiness will always be a little sadness, within our difficulties some light always shines.

20

Full Circle

This entire journey began while I was living in Belmont Heights California in the summer of 1971. It is now the summer of 2016 and I have returned to Belmont Heights to live this final third period of my life. I have come full circle.

I began this journey as an ordinary young man loving life and what life has to offer. I then became someone with a purpose and mission to awaken all sentient beings and to deepen my own awakening endlessly. Having just had a dramatic brush with death from an enlarged or "big heart," as someone so aptly put it, I return with renewed vigor, happy and fulfilled, an ordinary elderly man, loving and appreciating this most precious life as never before. I am now ready both to carry on this mission and to die if it is my time, without fear of either life or death. I can say that I have found what I was searching for and, just as easily, that I found absolutely nothing.

Back in 1971 when I arrived at a small rustic cabin in the Santa Margarita Ranch ten miles north of San Luis Obispo, I began writing a book that I titled, "You Walk Alone." The first sentence was, "You are born alone and you die alone." Forty-five years later, in June of 2016, the truth of this statement resonated deeply with me when I was living once again in San Luis Obispo and I was so ill I thought I was dying. Unbeknownst to me, my heart had literally enlarged to the point that I was struggling to breathe and could barely move. I felt lonely and depressed, never more lifeless and completely alone.

I would walk the same streets I had walked so many years before, stopping to rest on every available bench, not knowing what was wrong with me. One day I was sitting in exactly the same spot where I used to sit begging for small change, watching a beautiful young homeless man probably 26 years old panhandling as I did back then. I considered going up to him and giving him some words of wisdom about life — when I realized I had absolutely no wisdom to offer. This struck me as so funny I had to laugh.

After forty-five years I knew nothing and had nothing to say to this homeless young man. He will live his journey and in forty-five years he may have some wisdom to share, or not. Knowing how our path is going to unfold is not it, in fact it would take all the beauty and mystery out of this great journey or, to use a less politically correct term, this trip.

"Dennis," my mother said to me back in '71, "you are just on a trip and some day you will come off it like all the other trips you've been on." "No Mom," I said, "this trip is endless." She was right; and yet so was I. This trip that I have been on for the past forty-five years seems in some way to have come full circle, and yet it goes on endlessly.

21

Air

I am the Air that you breathe in and out thousands of times a day,
that you continuously take for granted.
Without me you could not live.
Without me you would die a quick and painful death.
Even when you follow me in and out,
rarely do you identify with me and become me.
You keep your illusion of distance and separation,
but are you not me?
When you are me you disappear,
and all illusion of separateness goes too.
You call me breath, as if I were yours,
as if everything revolves around you.
I am not yours any more than you are mine.
I am what gives life to all things, inanimate as well as animate,
and what ends all life too, eroding and causing decay.
Eventually I give and take all life.
I belong to no one and no one belongs to me;
we are all connected and dependent on one another.
Your next breath, remember me.
I am here for you.

Glossary

The following abbreviations are used: Chin., for Chinese; Jap. for Japanese; and Skt. for Sanskrit.

Anuttara Samyak Sambodhi (Skt.) Supreme unsurpassed awakening or wisdom.

Arhat (Skt.) Originally a title given to people of high spiritual achievement, it was applied by the early Buddhists to one who had eliminated all defilements and had "no more to learn."

Bankei Yotaku (Jap. 1622-1693) Best known for his teachings on the Unborn Buddha Mind.

Baso Doitsu (Chin. Ma-tsu Tao-I, 709-788) Chinese Zen Master noted for his use of numerous training methods; famous for many sayings and incidents now incorporated into koans.

Bodhi-Mind The mind in which an aspiration to enlightenment has been awakened.

Bodhidharma (Skt.; Jap. Daruma; ca. 6th century) The twenty-eighth Dharma descendent of Shakyamuni Buddha, who brought Zen from India to China, where he became known as the First Patriarch.

Bodhisattva (Skt.) Literally, "enlightened being;" one who practices the Buddha Way and compassionately foregoes final enlightenment for the sake of helping others become enlightened.

Buddha (Skt.) Literally, "awakened one;" the historical Buddha, Shakyamuni; enlightened persons who have attained Buddhahood; the essential truth, the true nature of all beings.

Buddha-Dharma (Skt.) The true realization of life; the Way to follow in order to attain that realization according to the teachings of Shakyamuni Buddha.

Buddhayana (Skt.) See Yana.

Daisan (Jap.) See Dokusan.

Dharma (Skt.) The teachings of Shakyamuni Buddha; Truth; Buddhist doctrine; universal law.

Dharmas (Skt.) Phenomena; elements or constituents of existence.

Diamond Sutra (Skt. *Vajracchedika Sutra*) A text highly regarded by the Zen sect, it sets forth the doctrines of sunyata and prajna.

Dogen Kigen Zenji (1200-1253) One of the greatest masters in the history of Zen, he brought the Buddha-Dharma from China to Japan and is considered the founder of the Japanese Soto school.

Dokusan (Jap.) Interview between Zen student and Master (Roshi) in which the student's understanding is probed and in which the student may consult the teacher on any matters arising out of practice. Interview is with a Zen Teacher (Sensei) is called Daisan.

Emptiness (Skt. *sunyata*) The fundamental nature of all phenomena.

Ganto Zenkatsu (Jap.; Chin. Yen-t'ou Chuan-huo, 828—887) One of Tokusan's successors and a close Dharma brother of Seppo.

Genjokoan (Jap.) Literally, "Enlightenment Appears in Everyday Life;" one of the best-known fascicles of *Shobogenzo* by Dogen Zenji.

Glassman, Bernie Tetsugen Roshi (b. 1939) First Dharma successor of Maezumi Roshi, receiving Inka in 1995. Co-founder of Zen Peacemakers.

Hakuin Ekaku Zenji (1686-1769) A Patriarch of Japanese Rinzai Zen, systematized koan study as we know it today.

Harada Daiun Sogaku Roshi (1871-1961) One of the most important Zen teachers of modern Japan, trained in Soto and Rinzai traditions; teacher of Yasutani Roshi.

Hinayana (Skt.) See Yana.

Hyakujo Ekai (Chin. Pai-chang Huai-hai, 720–814) Established early set of rules of Chinese Chan monastic training, teacher of Obaku.

Inka (Jap.) In Soto Zen, "final seal of approval," conferring independence as a teacher with the title of Roshi.

Joshu Jushin (Chin. Chao-chou Ts'ung-shen, 778-897) One of the most important Chinese Zen Masters, a Dharma successor of Nansen, famous for his capacity to awaken students with brief verbal responses.

Kanzeon (Jap., also Kannon or Kan Ji Sai Bosa; Skt. Avalokitesvara; Chin. Kuan-yin) Literally, "the one who hears the sounds and cries, of the world;" the embodiment of compassion, one of the principal Bodhisattvas in Zen.

Karma (Skt.) The law of cause and effect.

Kensho (Jap.) Literally, "seeing into one's nature;" an experience of enlightenment, also known as satori.

Koan (Jap.; Chin. Kung-An) Literally, "public document;" in the Zen tradition, given by the teacher to bring students to realization and help them clarify their understanding.

Koryu Osaka Roshi (1901-1985) Japanese Rinzai Master and lay teacher from whom Maezumi Roshi received confirmation (*Inka*) in 1972.

Maezumi Taizan Roshi (1931-95) One of a first Japanese Zen Masters who brought Zen to the West; founder of the Zen Center of Los Angeles (ZCLA).

Mahakashapa (Skt.) Became the Dharma successor of Shakyamuni Buddha when he alone smiled as Buddha silently held up a flower; took over leadership of the Sangha after Buddha's death.

Mahayana (Skt.) See Yana.

Mumonkan (Jap.) *The Gateless Gate*, a mjaor collection of koans produced by Mumon Ekai (1183-1260).

Nansen Fugan (Chin. Nan-ch'uan P'u-yuan, 748-835) One of the great Chinese Zen Masters of the T'ang period, Dharma successor of Baso and teacher of Joshu.

Nirvana (Skt.) A non-dualistic state, the original meaning of which was "to extinguish or burn out for lack of fuel," implying the complete exhaustion of all ignorance and craving. Sometimes refers specifically to the state of profound enlightenment attained by Buddha.

Paramitas (Skt.) Literally, "gone to the other shore." The paramitas are a natural expression of the enlightened mind, the mind of meditation.

Patriarch Title applied to Dharma successors who have received and formally transmitted the Buddha-Dharma from Shakyamuni Buddha through twenty-eight generations in India and six in China down to Daikan Eno, the Sixth Chinese Patriarch. Since then, Dharma transmission has not been limited to one successor, so all who have received formal transmission are termed Patriarchs. Also, Ancestor, Dharma-successor.

Prajna (Skt.) Enlightened wisdom; wisdom that transcends duality of subject and object.

Precepts (Skt. sila; Jap. kai) Buddhist teachings regarding personal conduct, which can be appreciated on a literal level as ethical guidelines and more broadly as aspects or qualities of reality itself.

Rinzai Gigen (Chin. Lin-chi I-hsuan, d. 866) One of the great masters of the T'ang dynasty in China and the founder of the Rinzai school of Zen, noted for its emphasis on enlightenment and use of koans in zazen practice. Rinzai was a Dharma successor of Obaku.

Roshi (Jap.) Literally, "old teacher;" an older Zen Master; in the Soto tradition, a seasoned Master at least fifty-two years old.

Samadhi (Skt.; Jap. zanmai) A state of mind characterized by one-pointedness of attention; a non-dualistic state of awareness.

Samsara (Skt.) Literally, "stream of becoming;" the experience of suffering arising from ignorance reflected in the condition of our usual daily life.

Sangha (Skt.) Originally referring to the community of Buddhist monks and nuns, later came to include laypersons who have received the precepts. In Zen, the term also connotes the harmonious interrelationship of all beings, phenomena, and events, the inseparability and harmonious working of Buddha-Dharma.

Satori (Jap.) See Kensho.

Sawaki, Kodo Roshi (Jap,. 1880-1965) teacher of Kosho Uchiyama Roshi, known as "homeless Kodo."

Sensei (Jap.) Title meaning teacher. In Soto Zen, one who has received Dharma transmission.

Seppo Gison (Jap.; Chin. Hsueh-feng I'ts'un, 822-908) Chinese Zen Master, successor of Tokusan and Dharma brother of Ganto.

Sesshin (Jap.) Literally, "to collect or settle the mind;" an intensive silent Zen meditation retreat.

Shakyamuni (Skt.) Literally, "the sage of the Shakya clan;" Siddhartha Gautama, the historical Buddha.

Shiho (Jap.) Dharma transmission, whereby a Zen student becomes a Dharma successor, with the title Sensei. See Patriarch, Transmission.

Shikantaza (Jap.) Literally, "just sitting;" refers to zazen itself, without supportive devices such as breath-counting or koan study.

Sixth Patriarch (Chin. Hui-neng; Jap. Eno, 638-713) Traditionally said to have been illiterate, he was enlightened while still a layman upon over-hearing a recitation of the Diamond Sutra. He became the Dharma suc-cessor of the Fifth Patriarch, Hung-gen, and all lines of Zen now existing descend from him.

Soto School The Zen lineage founded by Zen Masters Tungshan Liang-chieh (Jap. Tozan Ryokai, 807-869) and Ts'aoshan Pen-chi (Jap. Sozen Honjaku, 840-901). The Japanese branch was founded by Zen Masters Dogen Kigen (1200-1253) and Keizan Jokin (1268-1325).

Sutra (Skt.) Literally, "a thread on which jewels are strung;" Buddhist scripture; a dialogue or sermon attributed to Shakyamuni Buddha and to certain other Buddhist teachers.

Sunyata (Skt.) See Emptiness.

Suzuki, D. T. (Jap. Daisetz Teitaro Suzuki, 1870-1966) One of the best known interpreters of Zen in the West. Trained in Zen as a layman and was primarily interested in the intellectual interpretation of Zen teaching.

Suzuki, Shogaku Shunryu Roshi (1905-1971) Japanese-born founder of San Francisco Zen Center and Tassajara monastery, author of *Zen Mind, Beginner's Mind*.

Tao (Chin.; Jap. do) Literally, the "Way," or "Path".

Tathagata (Skt.) Literally, "thus coming, thus going," indicating the enlightened state, or "suchness;" one who has attained supreme enlight-enment on the Way of Truth; one of the ten titles of the Buddha.

Teisho (Jap.) A formal talk by a Zen Master on a koan or other Zen text. It is non-dualistic, which distinguishes it from an ordinary discursive lec-ture on a Buddhist topic.

Theravada (Pali) Literally "teaching of the elders," school of Buddhism based on the early teaching of the Buddha, widely practiced in S.E. Asia.

Third Patriarch (Chin. Chien-chih Seng-t'san; Jap. Kanchi Sosan, d. 606) Author of the poem *Hsin Hsin Ming*, Verses on the Faith Mind.

Tokusan Senkan (Jap.; Chin. Te-shan Hsuan-chien, 781?-867) A most influential teacher, from whom nine major Zen Masters received Dharma transmission. Famous for the compassionate severity of his training: "Thirty blows if you speak, thirty blows if you do not!"

Tozan Shusho (Jap.; Chin. Tung-shan Shou-chu; 910-90) Chinese Zen Master famous for his Five Ranks or Stages of the Way. Dharma-successor of Ummon.

Transmission Also Dharma-transmission (Jap.; Shiho). The "seal of approval" handed down from Buddha to Mahakashyapa and through each successive generation of ancestors to the present. People who have received Dharma-transmission from an authentic lineage-holder are called by various titles, including Ancestor, Patriarch, and Dharma-successor.

Ummon Bun'en (Jap.; Chin. Yun-men Wen-yen, 864-949) One of the most important Chinese Zen Masters and among the first to use the teachings of preceding teachers in a systematic way as part of Zen training.

Upaya (Skt.) Skillful or expedient means, usually referring to skill in expounding the teaching, especially in accordance with the needs of the student.

Yakusan Igen (Jap.; Chin. Yaoshan Weiyan, 745–828), the Dharma great-grandson of the Sixth Patriarch.

Yamada Koun Roshi (Jap,. 1911-1989) Dharma-successor of Yasutani Roshi.

Yana (Skt.) Literally, "vehicle." The three yanas by which a practitioner can travel on the way to enlightenment. Hinayana, the Lesser Vehicle, corresponds to a literal interpretation of Buddha's teachings. Buddhayana or One Mind/One Body vehicle is the absolute or nondual perspective. Mahayana, the Greater Vehicle, is responding to each situation according to circumstances. It is the way of the Bodhisattva, who vows to liberate all sentient beings.

Yasutani Hakuun Ryoko Roshi (1885-1973) One of the first Japanese Zen Masters to teach in the West. He was trained in both Rinzai and Soto Zen traditions.

Zazen (Jap.) Literally, *za* means "sitting" and *zen* "meditation" or "samadhi;" the practice of Zen meditation.

Zendo (Jap.) A meditation hall for the practice of zazen.

Zenji (Jap.) Literally, "Zen Master;" a title applied to the head of each Zen school; a term of great respect given to the most renowned and accomplished Masters.

Zuigan Shigen (Jap.; Chin. Jui-yen Shih-yen, 9th century) Chinese Zen Master famous for his personal meditation practice in which he would ask himself, "Master, are you in?" and then reply, "Yes, I am!"

D. Genpo Merzel was born in Brooklyn, New York, in 1944, and grew up in Southern California where he was a champion swimmer and All-American water polo player. He received a Masters degree from the University of Southern California and was a lifeguard and school teacher for ten years before being ordained as a Zen Monk under Zen Master Taizan Maezumi in 1973. He became Maezumi Roshi's second Dharma Successor in 1980. In 1982 he began teaching independently throughout Europe, founding the International Kanzeon Sangha, now with Zen Centers in Salt Lake City, San Francisco and Seattle and internationally in the Netherlands, France, Poland, England, Germany, Belgium, Spain and Portugal. He received Inka, final seal of approval as a Zen Master, in both the Soto and Rinzai Zen traditions, from Roshi Bernie Glassman in 1996. From 1996-2007 he served as President of the White Plum Asanga, a worldwide community of the Dharma heirs of Maezumi Roshi and their successors. In 1999 he created the Big Mind Process, which is now taught and practiced through numerous disciplines worldwide. He has conferred Dharma transmission on sixteen successors and Inka on eleven Zen Teachers. He has two children, a son Tai Merzel, an aerospace engineer in Washington state, and a daughter, Nicole Merzel Rasmuson, a school teacher in Miami, Florida.